I'll find you in the dark because I'm the girl

who loves to stay lost amongst the midnight stars,

caught up with moonbeams in a lantern

trying to find my way back home.

Solo Works

Available at global online stores

Swallowing The Moon
Ballads from my heart

The Story Of 8
13 Reasons Why I Choose Love

The Last Leaf Of Autumn
Barefoot and falling, infinity is a number that has none to end

P E A R L
On A Summer Leaf

Book 1 of The Evolution Series

The Expanded Edition

REENA DOSS

An Ink Gladiators Press® Publication

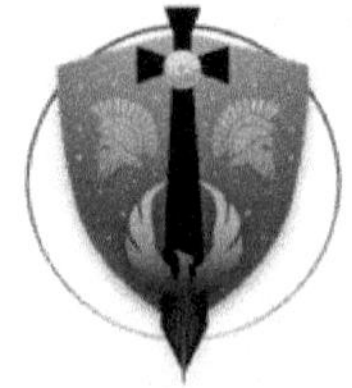

Ink Gladiators Press®
Publishing and promoting warriors on life's battlefield
Founded in 2019 | Bangalore, India
http://www.inkgladiatorspress.com/

Expanded Edition
ISBN-13: 978-93-90766-55-0

The first edition of this book was originally published in July 2021
and is a limited edition; ISBN - 13: 978-93-90766-25-3.

First Edition Editor: Shruti Sharma
Expanded Edition Editor: Ink Gladiators Press
Childlike Line Art Illustrations, Digital Paintings, Cover Art
& Book Design (with AI and photographic elements):
Leonie Belle Hawk

No one else can fill me with happiness except you, **my beloved Weaver Of The Celestial Sky.** Thank you for teaching me everything I know and for instructing me every day on how to love and be loved. Without your amazing grace in my life, nothing I am today would be possible.

No one else could have taken my wild heart and taught me how to see the world with gentle eyes except you, **my lovely Mystical Rose.** Thank you for always keeping your promise to be with me.

No one else could have given me the training I needed to be the person I want to continue being today except you, **my first home.** Thank you for my first lessons in love and for the places where I discovered how to determinedly add love in a boiling kettle filled with imagination, kindness and encouragement.

No one else in the whole world could have shown me that Heaven was real except you, **my little brother.** Your short life span puzzled me when I wondered about your purpose until I realized that it meant so very much to me.

No one else could have found the layers of love that the old versions hid under layers of grief except for **the home I found within me.** Now, that they all know, they can keep choosing to shine in freedom from the chains that used to hold me back.

No one else can ever understand the power of dreams when they are good, placed in your heart for a purpose and which reveals themselves at the right time except for **the prayers I make about my future home.**

Thank you in advance to **the love of my life** whom I have not met but know in my soul is on his way to me. You are my promise—my gift of faith in what I have held sacred and yearned to receive throughout the years. I'm so glad that you exist because you are the mirror to the home within me.

And for you, dear Reader:

No one else can make me feel visible
in the ways that you do when you read my ink.

Thank you for finding pearls under my bleeding heart.

Thank you for choosing a page in my world.

Thank you for keeping me.

PEARL ON A SUMMER LEAF

Does your heart know the sound of its beat? Did your heart ever forget how it spoke when silence was all the space it was given? Do you know how your heart could die when you stop it from singing its songs?

Pearl On A Summer Leaf is the first part of the autobiographical collection of memoirs in The Evolution Series where Reena Doss dives into the oceanic stories of her past to collect stars hidden under the dark narrative sky of her scars.

As you turn each page, the author gives you a glimpse into different stages of her early growth, perceptions and observations and shows you how every part of your history, no matter how small or big or wounded, has greater significance if you can bring what is unfathomable up to the surface, laugh as they transform into pearls and dance boldly into the light with them.

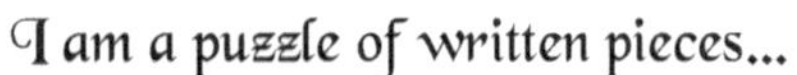

I am a puzzle of written pieces...

The POET in me broke free of the writer

and spilled STARS on a white sky

scattered and spaced across like the MILKY WAY

...in a white paged sky

Under A Bleeding Heart

I stopped numbering my pages.
Infinity seems to be a better number and my story is still unwritten.
Besides, I do like its symbol a lot—a sleeping ∞

The Limited Edition
Reviews from Goodreads and Amazon

Striking personal poetry that bleeds with love, faith, and wisdom.

There is no ready-made recipe for finding your voice and using it, consistently and selflessly, for writing a poetry collection that would captivate readers. Writing an autobiography in a poetic form seems a double daunting task because of the fears to be exposed for judgment from total strangers and fears to be overwhelmed with words, willing to escape from within. Squeezed between two opposing sides, one has to take a leap of faith.

Pearl On A Summer Leaf: An autobiographical collection (The Evolution Series Book 1) is the first book in the series, depicting a very personal journey by Reena Doss. Using a balanced, elegant blend of prose and poetry, the author describes her life from birth until she was 15 in three parts, each revolving around one idea. 'Birth,' 'Sheltered,' and 'Cracked' contain themes of family, love, faith, kindness, compassion, thoughts on being a girl and then a woman in modern India. Despite the autobiographic nature of the book, the topics it raises go beyond the categories of merely personal experience, thus allowing people far away from India and with different backgrounds to connect with the author's words.

Some topics like child abuse and sexual harassment are so uncomfortably raw that they hurt, even if one hasn't encountered them himself/herself. Each poem (if it can be named so) consists of a little snippet of the author's life and ends with a short poetic note. As the author reveals in the 'Acknowledgments' section, she deliberately postponed the publication, following her uncle's advice. Retrospect helped the author to see her experiences in a new light. Her poetic notes are full of wisdom and vulnerability.

Reena Doss

"Hope requires no lessons in learning; it grows with each passing moment when its wings are free."

"The many maybes are a casket of funeral flowers."

"Trauma culminates to a crescendo in the unlikeliest of memories."

Summarizing my review, I can say that Reena Doss's book would be an ideal addition to any poetry lover's collection.
—Darya Silman @darya_silman on Instagram
Poet, Writer & Reviewer of over 350+ reviews

Pearl On A Summer Leaf is a wonderfully written beginning to Reena Doss's autobiographical series.

It is immensely engaging, refreshing and an endearing easy read. I look forward to the second volume at some point.

I would definitely recommend this book.
—Mrinalini Aryan @mrinalini8612 on Instagram
Artist, Reader & Reviewer

This is an endearing true-life story of a young lady with the sweetest soul that I have ever met who has now become a dear friend in my heart. I've enjoyed reading *Pearl On A Summer Leaf* very much. I'm very impressed and attracted by Reena's style of writing. Reena is a naturally talented storyteller. I was drawn into her world and feel her pain and joy as though I was a spectator right beside her at her becoming of age journey.

A few poignant chapters pained and angered me at the abuses that this lovely young girl has encountered and drew concern and a sense of protectiveness for her. Conversely, some light-hearted chapters and episodes warmed my heart that she is so well-loved by her family and vice-versa. Through her eyes and entrancing narration, I have come to love her charming family members as much as Reena has.

This is a worthwhile read over a warm cup of tea to appreciate the warmth of God's unconditional love and irreplaceable family bond and support in the author's life.

—Geraldine Steele @carmennation_tan2 on Instagram
Poet, Writer and Reader

Pearl on a Summer Leaf **is the kind of book that draws you in** with its powerful storytelling, as the author gives you glimpses of her life that draw out emotions that are universal in their relatability.

Filled with a wonderful mix of simplicity that charms, depth that grips, and memorable lines that invite a reread, it's the kind of impactful writing that will linger in your mind long after you have finished reading it.

I'd wholeheartedly recommend this book to any and all lovers of the written word.

—Shruti Sharma @shrutiscapes on Instagram
Poet, Photographer and Author of Monsoon Tales *and* Poetscapes

Reena Doss

This book is an honest and heartfelt rendition of emotions and memories of the author's childhood and formative years.

The flow of words is beautiful. It is a journey, which takes the reader into the world of the author's past.

I read the Kindle version of this book. A sentimental book.
—*Rupali Gore @rupalidilipgore on Instagram*
Poet, Writer & Author of Calms and Balms

The Expanded Edition

A deeper dive into the psyche of generational trauma

Rereading the first edition while working on this expanded version has shown me how important it is to encourage those fighting for their stories to be heard. We have to own our voices, especially if we find ourselves stuck in other people's narratives, being asked to sew our mouth shut or being discouraged from speaking up just because the truth of your experiences doesn't sit well with them.

Our voices stay silent because they have become so enmeshed with false loyalty ties that they do not know how to break free. There is only one way out of the chaos. **We must feed that underlying need to use the gifts, talents and abilities you were given and that feel natural and easy to do.** When you use them—you will be honoring your freedom, exercising your right to exist in this world and which ultimately becomes a realization of your purpose.

Most generations (whether past or present) cannot accept accountability for past actions that have not been the best ones. While they should have been more focused on fostering the components of love, they were busy speaking life to the death patterns of those before them. This is because they are stuck in the pattern of needing to be right and what that does is it blocks growth, it refuses to apologize and it won't allow pride to take a backseat. In retrospect though, not many of us have the courage to take the time to heal the linked traumas of the past and present within. We will often choose to push them away, focus on the rat race goals that the world has set for us, rather than put aside time to work with the Weaver and allow Him to lead us into the areas or versions of self that get caught in cycles that choose to accept love that does not come from Him.

When you deny or do not speak up about the bad or evil that happened to you— whether by known people or strangers—their demons will use your unhealthy ideas of what love is to remain or make a house within you and thus, the next generation (whether you have children or not) will get influenced by the way you live your life and will have the arduous task of choosing to break the cycle or continue it. I have observed different generations' fight (against their innocence) while they struggle with this dilemma for most of their lives. They think they are being loyal, that they are choosing to love like their faith says they must and so therefore, their voices need to remain quiet in order to be accepted within familiar toxic cycles they themselves hate being in.

This is because this is what they believe love is and thus, they refuse to operate outside of it or explore healthier ways. These are the generations that get stuck, living under the assumptions that they are respecting (on the surface) those who once represented exalted positions in their life. However, there is a difference between respecting what is good and converting people into idols of worship.

You won't believe how common it is to hear those deeply emotional, passionate and sensitive men and women refer to those they highly look up to in the form of idolatry. Completely unaware of their deep underlying issues, they will say, for example: "He/She is a god/goddess to me because they did this and this and that and that." (To clarify: I am not referring here to a healthy appreciation for historical mythology or different cultures with the intent to emulate or recognize traits, habits or behaviors in people; instead, I am pointing out the unspoken pitfall hidden in the folly of converting people you love into idols that elevate them to a level that has no room for their humanity, thus destroying its very qualities). That is a transactional pattern of loving and is a hundred percent unhealthy. This is wrong for many reasons but I'll point out three important ones for you to reflect on. First of all, you are making them responsible for being your mirror of self-worth. Secondly, when you equate a human being to the level of God Himself, you have actively chosen what love is not. Thirdly, the moment that person falls from your designated pedestal, your entire world will shatter because human beings by nature are very flawed.

A healthy way of choosing to love those we look up to, admire and respect is by giving them the space to be imperfect, to make mistakes and to be allowed the strength to be weak. This is what frees the false chains of attachment in your relationship with them, breaks down your ideas of expectations and creates a momentum of safe exploration to discover who they are, rather than choosing what you want to see to love. If you ever find yourself in the throes of a people-pleasing addiction, then know that what you are allowing to happen is far deadlier than going with the flow to keep the peace of others, while simultaneously destroying your own.

The roots of darkness that may have succeeded in making a home within you, will gain traction to dig deeper into the heart of you if you block the pain of what they are doing while you are pretending they don't exist. This is when you will involuntarily project a false light because your real light is being forced into hiding. So instead of blocking their existence and thinking that they can't touch you—turn around, catch hold of them, face their truth in the light and then, convert that hurt you hide by giving it its freedom through the gifts of writing, art or other creative avenues that you were born with.

This will not only be a victory for you, but for those who unknowingly and knowingly gave those scars to you. It is also for those strangers passing by who need your testimony for their own situations in life to make sense.

The point of breaking the strings of unhealthy attachments is easy because it is already broken. It is the journey to realize this reality which is the tough part. Learn to accept who you are and let go of trying to fix those parts in others. Stop being a vessel of emotional supply to house others' blame, shame and guilt, especially when they are choosing to block feeling it all for themselves. Discern how to differentiate between being accountable for what are your mistakes and saying no to the habit of accepting what isn't yours to carry. Refuse the pattern of needing to earn love. Empty yourself to make space for the path that is yours. Focus on being more you. These steps will take every ounce of your effort till you reach that tipping point. Sometimes, it will be a lifelong struggle but don't despair because as long as you are trying, the path of unlearning a bad pattern eases into a good one. You will find yourself able to move forward until you come face to face with the next battle.

All these little steps forward, paradoxically, repel the ones who cannot see your value when you are of no use to them. They will be the ones who will demand you go back to how you used to be through a series of chaotic storms that you will be shocked you had to walk into to get to the other side. They will be the ones who distance themselves and view you with narratives that make themselves feel better about why they are treating you the way they are. They are the ones who will abandon you when you are going through hell. But don't be disheartened, these are the temporary hard parts you will need to be prepared for because you will have to face the excruciating heartbreak of the lies you told yourself existed when they didn't. **There will be no lullabies to comfort you except your fire, your courage and your soul.**

There will be strangers who will come to drain the poison of what you swallowed so let them. There will also be the unexpected that you will discover at the end, which you will not regret finding because joy is what you deserve. Sometimes, you will also get the opportunity to rebuild your relationships from a healthier standpoint but this only happens if you are willing to be brave enough to walk away from the old ways because you know you are worthy of it. Sometimes, you will have to be patient for others to catch up to your level of letting go, healing and growth. Sometimes, you will have to be ready to accept that some relationships may not change. Then and only then, does loving from a distance become a must. **No being is born bad.** They become what they choose to follow, hide or suppress.

When the Weaver lights up your higher calling after allowing you to walk through the desert of pain, desolation and suffering, you will know exactly what to do. Most people deny hearing this instinctive calling because they are afraid of all the implications it will bring. They choose to lock their feelings, dreams and passions and get stuck in the so-called requirements that make their little worlds of comfortable validation feel secure, even when they know subconsciously that it is all an illusion.

To live is to follow your soul's calling, which in turn teaches the physical heart to open itself to beat freely for the Weaver. If you stop the heart, you die because its very nature is to give the body the fuel it needs from the first breath that gave us His and which proclaims with its existence—**"YHWH"—Yes to His will,** whether your mind accepts this truth while being attacked by lies or if your spirit feels poorly.

I would not be here needing to write all of this, needing to bring to light what isn't spoken in the shadows and needing to shed what isn't mine, even at the cost of losing all those who might misunderstand my reasons, have misunderstood my memoirs and will misread my intentions. It took me more than eleven years to realize that my peace is more about doing what is right in the eyes of the Weaver than about pleasing any human being.

Prayer is a deadly weapon. Do not underestimate its powerful protection over the mind. It will expel many a fog during transitions. Use it as often as you need.

Scribbles

A note from the author

Dear Reader,

Thank you so much for being here. Thank you for stepping into these long forgotten realms. Thank you for choosing to open this door inside my heart, for visiting its sacred rooms and for listening to a voice that once felt lost.

I find it extremely liberating to reclaim my first voice along with the others by breaking their dams so that they can join the visible ocean to be felt, seen and heard. The past carries lessons for the present as well as the future and we must face it all with courage if the chief objectives for our journey includes forgiveness, reconciliation and letting go to make space for the new.

Pearl On A Summer Leaf details the metamorphosis stages of a Pearl in an oyster being slowly shaped into who I was constantly becoming. These are memoirs captured inside this time capsule and are retold in written form from my perspective so as to provide an account of events that took place prior to my birth till the end of my 15th year. They are not completely placed in the order of occurrence but that's because memories are exactly like that.

I hope you enjoy reading the embedded stars of my soul. I pray that you will treat my voices kindly and keep them safe. I am always on the journey of becoming…upon the path that will lead me home.

May the quill of Hope always find you in the dark,

Reena Doss

Dated: Till you find pearls under your own bleeding heart

The Map Of My Heart

The map of my heart is why I add love through the voices I was given in adversity

Reena Doss

The map of my heart is a tapestry of colors, worlds, and mysterious beauty, reminiscent of the silver moon against the night sky. The paths I've taken have been marked by broken roads, but I've enjoyed revisiting them to watch wildflowers bloom in the gaps. I find joy in sowing new seeds of beauty on those same paths, especially when life teaches me a new lesson from places I initially missed. I then strive to transform and improve by altering my patterns, bit by bit. Over time, I've discovered that some paths follow me instinctively, once I've learned the truth about them, instead of me chasing them to solve who they are. It was then that I realized that for someone to find my heart, they must always follow the wildflowers that grew as my stories wove themselves together on my journey.

The map of my heart is a leaf with roots that reveal who I am, who I've become, and who I will keep choosing to be. To know me is to know the ocean of secrets and that is impossible for the tides love her too well to disclose who she is, even as she defies the sky's gravity and travels to meet the depths of the waters she is loyal to.

The map of my heart is like a pearl and that's why only the moon knows my story for all its pieces found the Sun's stars and they know we became whole because of it.

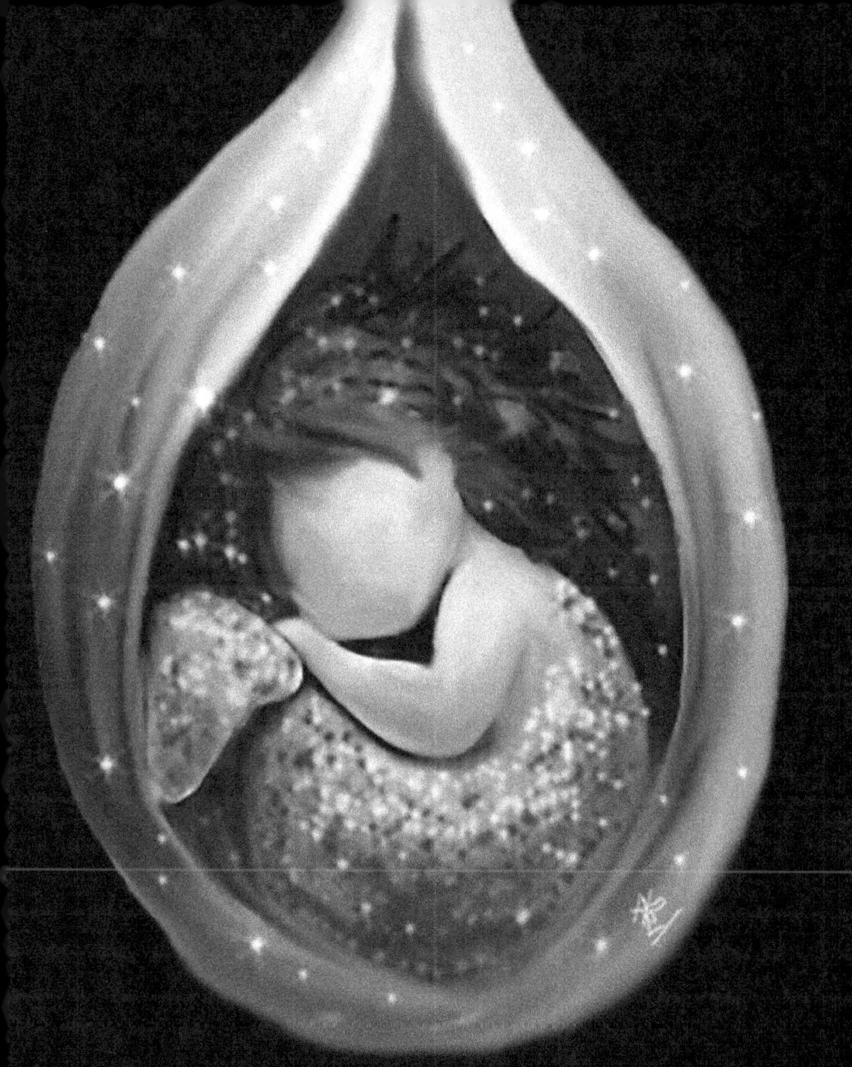

I

BIRTH

Birth is another word for hope;
a forerunning testament in a life that is beginning.

Hello

Unseen
unheard
unknown
dreamed of
not shaped yet
conceived
born into
existence—
a crescent moon…

Aware and yet unaware
finding the ocean
and soaking
inside the newness
of feelings

Meticulously planned
by the Weaver
to start out as
a Pearl sac
and to say at last,
I   a m

invisible

h e r e

The wheels of a Hero Majestic witnessed their story under twilight's stars when the dragon plucked up courage to ask a mermaid if she'd be his.

Nine years, family friends, two different paths joined while pursuing the truth in the light after shadows. South and East joined hands like an upside down L on the rugged, complicated Indian map.

Many crosswords later, Bangalore and Calcutta found dreams in their ninth year.

Eyes were opened to see what they'd sought—Love had been there before them all along.

South and East state lines were not at fault

She'd waited so long to be found—39 years already, set in her ways under the ocean, when the shy dragon appeared to suddenly dive in and break the spell.

The dragon knew in his heart that she was given to him in this life to never be apart, so onward he plunged like an excited hurricane—madly in love, fearless, and full of hope in the magic of his faith.

Uncertainty glimmered in the mermaid's eyes; she was 90 percent sure of this union.

"What about children?" she asked, anxious.

"Sarah and Abraham," was all he said and she dismissed long-held fears that weighed heavily on her chest, imbibed by the stigma of society and the unknown future.

The Weaver's providence was their building foundation; a choice to not rely on the understanding of things to come.

Accepting his hand, she rose from the waters, stretching her limbs, finding it strange to discover legs that ran toward love.

She tossed hair that gleamed of fire as the dragon opened his chest to give her his heart. She formed a decision to stick by him when she chose to walk upon the land.

Unprepared; commitment was a promise
witnessed by the timeless ocean and the shore

A world of struggles was a part of their legacy, for the kind of magic they exuded together was not according to the rules laid out by others, and those first years in Bangalore contained storms of disaster.

It was easy to speak of faith, but harder to live it when it seemed that the Weaver had forgotten them as they trudged through their start, finding joy in simple things, praying and hoping for better days.

Their convictions were tested at every twist and turn. Sometimes, family helped, but most times they frowned. With every turned up nose, the dragon and his mermaid experienced lost pride and dignity.

Problems; belief systems were tried in fire

The dragon could transform the elements and the mermaid could flow into any situation with ease and grace. A degree in civil engineering and teaching experience in the real world were not enough for them to find what they required to survive.

Though the dragon felt despair as the struggle hit close to home, he did not let go of his faith in the Weaver. Shifting from home to home, a baby on the way, bills to catch up on, and a hardworking wife who needed more rest and better food; more than he could afford to pay.

At every step of the way they tried to solidify a home, unaccustomed to cultural landscapes so different from what they'd known, and found failure could be washed away with laughter under the stars.

Times were rough and catching a break was tough.

Instability; education doesn't guarantee success, love does

The middle of Summer in the western world, but tropical India was in the thickest fall of Monsoon dreams.

Glorious showers of blessings poured down upon our part of the world at the end of the second week of July when the mermaid was rushed to the hospital amidst the wild torrential rains of Calcutta.

Death beckoned both—toxemia infecting the mermaid and the baby as the dragon paced back and forth, afraid…

Summer and rain; July was an excruciating labor of love

We could have died, but we were destined to survive.

The mermaid lay back at last, exhausted. The dragon sank down, breathing in his relief; for they'd heard my lusty battle cry, exultant in its arrival, determined to live.

I was born in Monsoon, discovered in the Indian Ocean—a Pearl in an oyster with almond shaped eyes and long hair that stuck out like a porcupine. The mermaid said my hair would tickle her when I moved or kicked. I like to think that I made her laugh with joy to know I was there.

I was a cesarean, cut open to step out; like cutting the ribbon at the start of something new, or trimming the garden for it to bloom, like separating the cords of dependency and comforting familiarity from the mermaid's womb.

I used to think that cesarean was spelled scissor-ian. Doesn't it make sense for a scissor to cut things open? It made perfect sense that a scissor brought me out into the unknown.

The Weaver had the astounding ability to transform us into a family. He did not fail their trust in Him but provided in perfect timing—an impossible dream, despite the turbulent storms.

Heart desires placed within us by the Weaver are beyond our human vision

The dragon chose my name.

In different cultures, *Reena* means different things. It transcends from *gem* to *joy, song, rebirth, calm waters, melody,* and *serene.*

The dragon and mermaid selected my second name, *Johanna,* meaning, *God's grace* or *God is gracious.* The name seems apt to me because they were not quite sure if the Weaver would bless them with children. It is special to me because it is linked to *St. Joan of Arc,* the warrior saint who ignited my desire to serve others with courage with all that I am in the light of love.

I did not realize how the Weaver was constantly weaving a tapestry that would be mine to unravel in the future.

Melody; everything connects under the Sun

The dragon's siblings were my godparents.

Both have always tucked me under their wings, spoiled me when I visited them, and were extremely proud of me when I achieved anything.

They also prayed over me whenever possible and sent me a chosen word either on my birthday or on a special occasion.

The Weaver blessed me with a circle of love

My uncle brought a wooden cross from Rome for me.

At the back of the beautifully painted cross were the penned words:

"To my dear Reena,
may you discover this cornerstone
in your life."

I did not think of it seriously until I eventually discovered the wisdom of this during the darkest time in my life as an adult. He did not know it at the time, but my uncle who is a priest had given me one of the most powerful gifts I have ever received at such a young age.

**Cornerstone; victory is attained only by surrendering
one's sufferings through the cross of Christ**

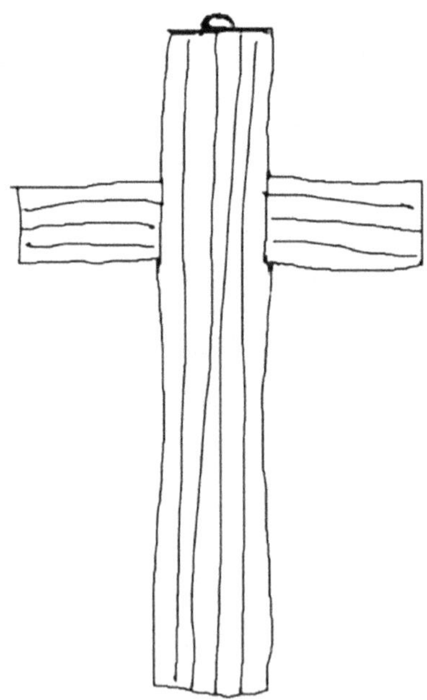

I was nearly one when the dragon brought two Lhasa Apso puppies to our first home in Bangalore. The dragon and mermaid loved dogs as this understanding of canines went way back to their own childhood years. I suppose that is why they wanted to share this experience with me as well.

He returned the golden brown one that same day. I don't think he consulted the mermaid on bringing two puppies home, but we did keep the black one. We named her *Twinkle* after my favorite nursery rhyme.

The dragon had to keep her at Grandy's home after I started crawling. Apparently, I kept trying to put any part of the puppy I could grab into my mouth. I played with her every time we were at Grandy's and later, when she was moved to my godmother's place.

Twinkle remained my dearest friend until the day she became a diamond star in the night sky, the year we both turned 12.

When you love a dog like a family member, they don't leave your heart

I was a year old when I was rushed to a hospital, running a high fever from an allergy. I didn't like leaving the dragon and mermaid's side to go to anyone so when they heard my screams when the nurses took me, they were beside themselves.

The tyrants wouldn't even let the mermaid come in.

This probably explains why I've disliked the smell of hospitals and been wary of white coats ever since.

Layers; We can sort through odd dislikes
by analyzing the past from the trunk we store in our minds

I liked walking around barefoot.

I enjoyed the way the cold marble or the warm wood felt and I would often get into trouble with the dragon and mermaid who took great pains to make sure we did not get sick by getting us slippers to wear in the house. This stricture was in vain, in my case.

Walking barefoot at home was something I liked.

The crescent felt the Earth call the oceans to dance with her feet

Reena Doss

The mermaid asked the dragon to bring down the clothes and nappies drying on the terrace and he went upstairs, leaving me behind. I loved going to the terrace because there was such freedom to be had in the open space, but I was forbidden from going there without one of them.

I knew the dragon had instructed me not to leave the house without my slippers on, but I couldn't find them and his slippers were readily available. I slipped them on and felt very grand as I climbed the steep stairs. As I reached the top stair, the dragon began to head downstairs with the huge bundle of clothes and didn't notice I was there. Startled by the bundle pushing me, I tried to move out of the way and slipped.

Shocked, helpless, and petrified, the dragon watched as I bounced on my head all the way to the bottom stair. The noise was so loud the mermaid came running, shouting my name, terrified.

The dragon dropped the bundle, raced down the stairs and picked me up. They didn't let me sleep that day because they were afraid I would lose consciousness. I had a big bump on my head that was cold with all the ice they kept applying.

I was very tired when they gave me a lecture about not trying to wear the dragon's slippers again.

I believe in guardian angels

My earliest memories are of the dragon making me giggle as he told tall tales woven with his grand imagination. He even handwrote a song about my smile which is one of my most treasured possessions.

When he would tuck me into bed, he would sing in his deep baritone *May the Good Lord Bless and Keep You* by *Jim Reeves* and *Hush Little Baby, Don't Say a Word* by the *King's Singers*. There were many others, but these two stand out more than all the rest.

The mermaid had a soft, beautiful voice and when she sang *Count Your Blessings* by *Guy Penrod*, I would dream of faraway lands. She would sing a lot of songs by *ABBA* too, which probably had some influence on my dream to visit their country one day. The way she would sing *Fernando* would draw out a melancholy in my soul I couldn't explain.

Food is the mermaid's love language and she enjoyed cooking for us. She would also make feeding time interesting by pretending that each spoonful of food was a different bird that wanted to fly into my mouth. I liked choosing them as I grew more familiar with their odd sounding names.

They were rich like that in extraordinary ways, and on days when I would get frustrated or angry with them, I'd pull out these memories and let them wrap me up with all their warm snugness.

Both of them inspired my imagination in different ways and encouraged me to live in worlds no one else could see.

Some songs are precious because they are linked to unconditional love

The mermaid bled a lot. It was a baby, not quite formed yet. We did not know if it was a boy or girl.

The mermaid called him *David*. Did you know *David* means *beloved by God?* I don't think she knew its meaning when she named him, but I'm so glad he's safe with the Weaver.

The dragon said we were blessed because the Weaver had given us someone to intercede for us. I didn't know what he meant back then.

I think of *David* when I look at the stars and wonder what he's doing up there. I hope he is happy and having fun. He is a rare pearl tucked safely in the cocoon of his oyster carried by his guardian angel into his forever home.

I often ask him to pray for us, especially when one of us needs it the most. It's comforting to know my little brother looks out for us in Heaven.

Beloved; the Weaver has a purpose for every life, no matter the length of its term

I did not like the purple cookie monster at first.

He was a leftover hand-me down figurine, only one inch in size. He looked a bit scary and not at all cute and cuddly like the other toys. His bright red tongue made him appear more intimidating, but I found him to be quite an interesting character. One day, I was upset about something and was crying and when I looked up, there he was—his bright eyes watching me without blinking and for some weird reason, his vibrant "I am here" presence made me smile. His expressions were not pretty, sad or miserable. Whoever made him understood the reality of life because they made me think about why being curious and cheerful were good things. He taught me to see behind the mask of what others called a monster.

I wondered why he was called the Cookie Monster for a long time until he finally made sense when I watched the *Sesame Street* show. I loved the characters of Big Bird, Ernie, Bert, Abby, Grover, and Elmo, but it was Count von Count and his obsession with numbers as well as the Cookie Monster with his mad love for cookies that would crack me up. Though the show made him blue, I was biased about my monster because nobody else wanted him.

I eventually lost him; he either disappeared or was given away. I'm not sure what happened, but later in life, when I remembered his tongue was always hanging out, I found myself giving him another name.

Purple Ide was always hungry

I kissed the mermaid's tummy.

My unicorn was in there, but I wasn't sure if she was going to be a boy or a girl. Doctors and hospitals don't reveal the baby's sex for fear of female infanticide that is quite rampant in India.

I remember feeling happy that I wasn't going to be alone anymore. The Weaver had heard my prayers, the ones I said every day with the mermaid and the dragon.

So, I kissed the mermaid's tummy once more just to let whoever was in there know I loved them already.

That's when I heard the kicking and I squealed with delight.

I was going to be a big sister.

Some moments are so magical in their start,
you can feel them take residence deep inside you

When she arrived in early February, I was going to be three.

She closed the Winter of our days with her first breath of Spring. Our world felt complete.

I was now a big sister and I was going to love, protect, and look out for her and beware anyone who tried to hurt her.

She looked so sweet, just like an angel sleeping.

Happy memories remain engraved without effort

She was a pain in the neck!

Why did she have to imitate me? It was so annoying. Doing everything I did, curious about what I was doing, and always wanting to be around me.

"Stop following me!" But she followed me.

"Stop copying me!" But she copied me.

"Stop repeating everything I say!" I would yell. "Stop repeating everything I say!" she would yell back, followed by her cheeky grin, which only served to infuriate me further.

If I could go back, I would say, "It's all right to follow, to copy and repeat anything and everything I say."

We were kids back then and I did not know how much she admired and looked up to me. Those moments now fill my heart with laughter and regret in equal measure.

My unicorn was still a baby and I was only a crescent

It wasn't easy at first, sharing the attention. I was quite selfish with my toys. Both of us wanted to be sure we got more than the other, but we just wanted to know we were loved equally.

When we planned mischief together, which would drive the dragon and mermaid nuts, we became the best of friends; especially if we were lucky enough to get away with it.

It is interesting to note that it would be better if you got lost in a desert or a pyramid in Egypt than attempt to understand why siblings alone are allowed to insult each other. Anyone else daring to enter this equation had better hope they have the right armor to leave in one piece.

Sharing, playing, and fighting together taught us a lot of life lessons we would need in social interactions. At the end of the day, when we yelled good night to each other, the dragon and mermaid, and everything under the sun just to extend our day, we found that love always, always remained.

It is a rare thing to know that no matter what happens, you can call the unicorn, knowing she's always got your back.

After all, we were going to be together forever.

No one else can know and understand you like your first playmate

The dragon thought it was a tailorbird at first.

While playing outside with the unicorn and Twinkle at Grandy's house, we noticed several odd-looking nests that looked like cones hanging from the bougainvillea tree and we asked the dragon excitedly what kind of bird made nests like that. The dragon told the unicorn to look at her famous bird book when we got home to be absolutely sure if it was a tailorbird.

The unicorn dashed off to open her prized book from the showcase, flipped through the pages and then pronounced triumphantly that it was a weaverbird. I was entranced by this knowledge and for some reason I did not forget this bird.

When I was older and had access to the library, I learned more about how the male of the species tried its best to construct the best home it could by putting in a lot of effort through the art of meticulous weaving in order for the female to choose him as her mate.

Later on in my teens, I thought about the weaverbird. It was its brilliant creativity that made me think of God and how He often plans everything so perfectly, despite my mistakes and shortcomings. When I looked up at the stars, they seemed to laugh as if I had discovered something that they had already known.

I smiled because I knew now who the true Weaver Of The Celestial Sky was

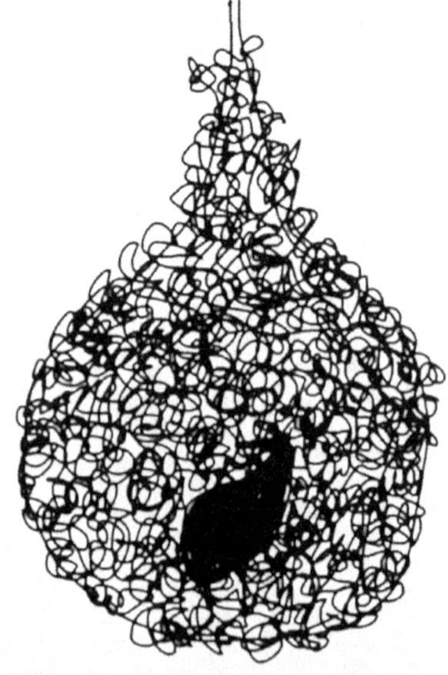

It was a rented premise of a shop that the dragon ran. I loved going there because it seemed to have everything, especially vanilla and strawberry ice cream (which was my favorite at the time).

The mermaid sometimes made the dragon's favorite cutlets to help generate sales. I loved the smells, the people and schoolchildren who came by to buy them for a quick lunch or snack. They would smile or have something kind to say.

The mermaid said I would stand outside like the sole proprietor of the shop as I ate my ice cream. The dragon used to say that the unicorn and I would ruin his business, but he was the one who would keep ice cream cups waiting for us.

Happy memories here at *Nik Nak Nook*.

Uncertainty fuels experience and teaches you to dive into more adventures

I taught my unicorn how to kiss the mermaid's tummy this time, just like she had taught me. I told her if we talked to the big belly, our sibling would hear us. So she did and I did and when we heard the baby kicking madly, we would grin at each other like we'd won a grand prize.

"How many kisses did you give the tummy?" one of us would ask and the other would yell back right away, "Infinity plus one over everything you say!"

Expecting life in a home is an event; a delightful season of waiting

The dragon prepared omelets in a hurry that morning. Then the three of us raced to the hospital.

The mermaid said some things that she shouldn't have but it set her up towards a path that she couldn't let go off down the road.

We feared the loss of the mermaid along with our baby. This was going to be her third cesarean and she was in surgery.

The dragon started praying and we prayed with him.

Hope requires no lessons in learning;
it grows with each passing moment when its wings are free

But the Weaver did the impossible once more when my baby dolphin joined us on that sunny day in April, bringing with her the sweetest Summer of our lives.

The unicorn and I took our roles very seriously as we gazed in awe at her; another unexpected gift from Heaven. In that moment, I knew that magic would continue to exist as long as hearts like ours knew how to let love expand.

The mermaid smiled at the dragon for they knew we were complete at last.

When baby dolphins make their appearance, the whole world laughs in joy

My baby dolphin gurgled a lot, babbling nonstop in baby gibberish. I often wondered what she was trying to say or if she was mad about something.

When she slept, she laughed so happily. I would worry something was wrong, but the mermaid told me that angels were talking to her.

I loved her toothless smile and the way she waved her hands in bubbly excitement whenever she saw one of us, wanting to tell us something very important. I wished I could speak her joyful baby babble.

I wanted to hear what she had to say.

Dolphins are radiant sunflowers

She wouldn't stop talking.

She would follow us around trying to tell us about each experience and what she thought about it.

"Get to the point!" we would often find ourselves telling her when her prolonged explanations grew to an hour and she would grow quiet and look forlorn as if we did not want to hear what she had to say. We did want to hear her stories, but why did she have to give us minute details on everything that happened? We were too impatient with her at times.

She would sulk then and wouldn't talk to us for hours. However, the dragon was the only one who could bring her back to her usual sunny self. I don't know how he did it, but she would start cracking up at something silly he would say or do.

She often found comedy in the little things, things that escaped us, and when she would start laughing, the whole world laughed.

She had that kind of gift—unique and special—for to be in her presence was to feel happy.

Love took on a different shape when she laughed

When our dolphin refused to sleep, the unicorn and I would tuck our stuffed toys around her so she'd feel cozy, while we danced and sang, making her quite dizzy and not succeeding in getting her to sleep.

We tried our best to help out when the dragon and mermaid were busy figuring things out—like how we would all survive, not worrying about dreams that were lost, sacrificing constantly for ours to take flight.

Family is layered in tones of love, sacrifice, and warmth

We lived in a twin house on that old street in Bangalore. It housed another family with three girls too.

They were older, with the youngest being closer to my age. We became the best of friends. The unicorn adored the eldest one and would run behind her shouting, "Thaaa," which was how her name ended, but Thaaa loved it. Their second one enjoyed carrying the dolphin around like a live doll.

The girls' folks were wonderful people; so kind and ready to help when the dragon was working and the mermaid was unable to constantly watch us with her broken leg. I loved this family so much.

When I started to notice the prejudice against Muslims as I grew up, I felt upset because their family had been a part of our family and labeling felt wrong.

Labels don't define people; they categorize them into a cycle of perpetual abuse

I treasure the memory of my Uncle bringing back twin bald dolls from Rome for the unicorn and me.

Our dolphin was still a baby, and when she slept, the unicorn and I would spend hours playing, fighting, and making up with these dolls as our constant companions.

In those days, we didn't have digital phones, so every Kodak roll with 36 precious photos was carefully filled with chosen moments. These memories are incredibly precious to me because they capture the essence of what I believed family, love, and happiness were.

Of course, as we grow up, we learn what works and what doesn't.

Writing has become my way of framing memories that didn't get photographed

A scorpion entered our home and crawled towards our sleeping area.

I'm unsure if it was afternoon or late evening, but I remember the dragon jumping up and making us move towards the wall. Before he could pick up the dolphin, the scorpion climbed over her sleeping face. We held our breath, afraid to startle it and trigger a fatal bite. Fortunately, the dolphin sleeps soundly and didn't wake up.

The mermaid removed her slipper and signaled us to remain silent. When the scorpion moved to the other side of the dolphin, the dragon quickly picked her up, and the mermaid fiercely beat the scorpion until it appeared to be dead. She then yelled at the unicorn and me to fetch a broom and dustpan. The dolphin woke up screaming, understandably upset at being disturbed at the commotion.

Apparently, scorpions can feign death and then sting their enemies quite viciously, so the mermaid carefully took it to the terrace and asked the dragon for his matchbox. As she lit a match and dropped it on the scorpion, it suddenly moved towards her, revealing its ruse.

Years later, I asked her how she knew that scientific fact, and she attributed it to something she had heard and seen as the way to kill poisonous creatures. I was impressed with this. I had admired her courage that day.

When did the mermaid's colors start to fade?

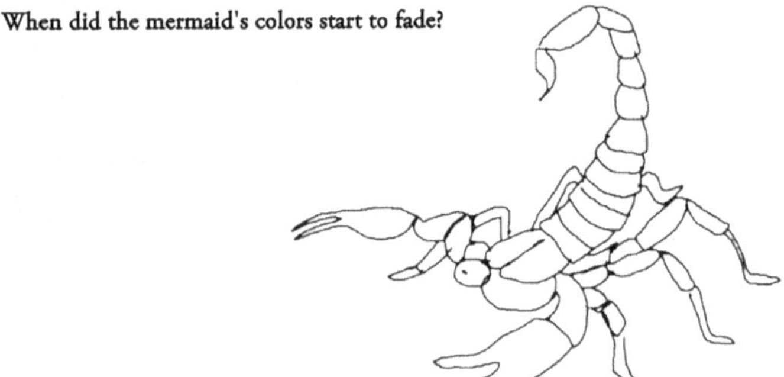

The dragon had a cassette player that he absolutely loved. He had recorded many moments of our growing years with it. It was the technology of our generation.

The mermaid disapproved of using our fists and foul language as we grew. "Use your words without trying to hurt each other," she'd say. It was the etiquette of our generation.

When they left us in charge one day for a few hours, we pulled out that recorder, pressed record, and happily used all the curse words we knew. The worst ones being, "Stupid, idiot, donkey, elephant, cow!" We played it back a number of times, pleased as punch with ourselves.

This was probably the only mischief the two of us pulled that we did not get into trouble for because it was not discovered.

We now recall this with great amusement—so much beautiful innocence in our childhood.

Mischief carried out successfully

Whenever we played "House, House," "Market, Market" or anything childish like that, the dragon was ready to be our extra playmate. We told him scornfully that he couldn't play with us 'cause he was an adult, but he would beg us and so we'd make him become our car, our donkey, our lion—well, you get the picture. Anything we asked him to be, he became with gusto, making us laugh till our bellies ached because he was far more entertaining.

When he would come back home, tired from work and lie stretched out on his front—ready to pass out—the three of us would run up and down his back. He did not get mad or chase us away. Instead, he would laugh and coin it "the best back massage of the highest quality."

Of course, it made us quite pleased with ourselves.

The dragon treated us like we were royal princesses
and that is something every girl should believe she is

The dolphin hated being left out, but we frequently did that to her when she carried tales to the mermaid about our misdeeds. So when we would get punished, we would tell her that we didn't want to play with her anymore.

Once we told her that she had been adopted and we'd not forget how heartbroken she looked that day. When she replied through tear-stained eyes, "It's okay if you don't love me because Jesus loves me", it made us both feel very ashamed of ourselves. We immediately apologized for our unkindness.

There was also an occasion where they ganged up on me. Though I forget the circumstances, I remember feeling quite heartbroken. When I asked them if they would be happy if I wasn't there, they said "Yes!" together. That made me so sad so I told them that when I was grown up, I would leave and they wouldn't be able to contact me.

They found that hilarious so they asked me where I would go when I didn't have anything. I hadn't thought it through so I quickly tried to cover up my hurt feelings by saying that I would marry a rich man and go live happily ever after in Australia. In my mind, that country felt quite far away and was an island so it felt appropriate to convey my deep feelings of rejection. That made them laugh harder. They could barely get their words out as they were rolling on the floor with amusement. "Okay! We'd help you pack!", they said and I walked away to hide my tears.

Looking back, that incident makes me chuckle but at that moment in the time, the pain I felt was real and the truth was, I was revealing a fear as well as predicting a reality where everything would change one day.

As children, we were sometimes mean without intending to be, but it was also in those moments that we learned how to watch our tongues. The rewards are always great when you choose to lead with love instead.

Being kind is a far more difficult route than pretending to be nice

Red, blue, yellow, white, and pink chickens.

The dragon got them for us in place of a puppy because our house was not suitable for keeping a dog. The mermaid insisted that if I wanted to keep them, I had to clean their cage every day, though she often helped me when I had a lot of homework. The unicorn and I were the most delighted and we played every day with them.

Eventually two died, an eagle grabbed one, and a cat took another.

A hawk injured the last one. We knew it would not survive. It became supper.

I cried because I knew this was the reality of life and I couldn't do anything about it.

**We can accept nature's lessons when we understand
that she cannot be tamed and caged for our pleasure**

The dragon had a special pen to mark our height on a piece of wood during our growing years. We were always so excited about learning how tall we had grown and would show off to each other.

I remained the tallest till we entered our teen years and then the unicorn shot up suddenly.

I was always the third shortest in my school years

The power cuts were frequent, especially during summer.

The unicorn, dolphin, and I would collectively sigh, unsure of how long we'd be without electricity. The dragon would light candles, and the mermaid and he would discuss things that seemed dull to us.

Meanwhile, we'd decide on our own entertainment.

In our younger years, we'd create silhouettes on the wall with our hands, challenging each other to guess what they were. As we grew older, we'd play dumb charades, sing, or spin tales.

In a child's mind, boredom is not an option

I recall burning my thigh twice.

The first incident occurred when we were seated at the round wooden table with the loose top (it wasn't attached to the base). I was impatiently waiting for my milk and banged the table with my fists, causing the glass with hot coffee to fall onto my right thigh. I likely screamed or howled, but I don't remember. The dragon acted swiftly and raced to the bathroom to submerge my burn in cold water. The mermaid applied medical cream and worried that I would have potential scarring. Fortunately, due to my young age, the burn healed over the years without leaving any lasting marks.

The second incident happened during bath time. We had to boil water in a large vessel since we didn't have access to hot water or a geyser. The mermaid typically bathed us before dinner and bedtime. As the unicorn and dolphin quarreled, distracting the mermaid, I asked if I could use soap foam to create a mermaid costume. In that moment, she accidentally poured hot water on my legs. I screamed and recoiled. Thankfully, the mug contained little water, and she was relieved she hadn't lifted it higher. We were all grateful the water wasn't scalding hot, and I didn't suffer any burns.

Following this incident, the mermaid deemed it time for me to bathe myself, which delighted me.

Growth occurs in stages, each beginning with a story

The dragon bought a table for me to study.

I loved it dearly and when I wasn't doing my homework, I would spend hours writing, sketching, and thinking about all the things I would do when I grew older.

It is now used as a water stand and I found myself teaching that part of me that wanted to hold on—to let it go.

I was sentimentally attached to that table for decades

There was a giant, ancient tortoise in the petting cage in the corner of the playground. I had nicknamed him King Louis because he looked so regal. He took his time to absorb and reflect on things. I thought him to be very wise. All my classmates seemed to love him, so why didn't they like me?

I didn't like it when a few of them kept hitting the cage trying to get him to move. A girl suddenly threw a stone directly at Louis, who immediately tucked himself into his shell. I was furious. When he peaked his head out again, she picked up another stone and my other classmates egged her on.

Not sure what to do, I grabbed her hand. She looked at me in confusion. "What?" she asked. "Don't", I said softly, "He's scared". She hesitated for a second, then shoved me roughly. I fell and she did it anyway.

"I'm sorry," I apologized to Louis as he cowered in his shell, hidden completely. I dusted the mud from my uniform, determination curving my fingers. I was going to be strong one day and I would protect those who couldn't fight back.

I told my unicorn about my plan to have a mansion that could house as many orphans and animals as we could fit into it. We agreed that that's what we would do when we grew up.

Later on, the school gave King Louis away to the zoo. I was glad though I was sad to see him go.

Resolution set in my chin and slid under my skin

She kicked me in the shin in class again and my eyes watered. I tried to kick her back, but it was half-hearted. I worried that I might hurt her. An odd smile flickered over her face as she deliberately pinched me hard. I yelped when I saw my skin had torn, but she laughed like it was a joke.

I told the mermaid when she asked about it. Angered, the dragon took it to the school authorities, but that only made things worse. Though I was separated from her, she did not stop finding opportunities to get to me.

I learned to keep quiet and took it until she got bored and moved on.

I drew a spider. I folded it neatly, ripped it into shreds, and threw it in the dustbin.

I drew a spider. I scratched it a hundred times until the paper tore.

I drew a spider. I gave it shoes and a hat and colored it in.

I gave it a handbag.

It was pretty.

**Art was the only constructive way I knew
how to transform the ugly into the beautiful**

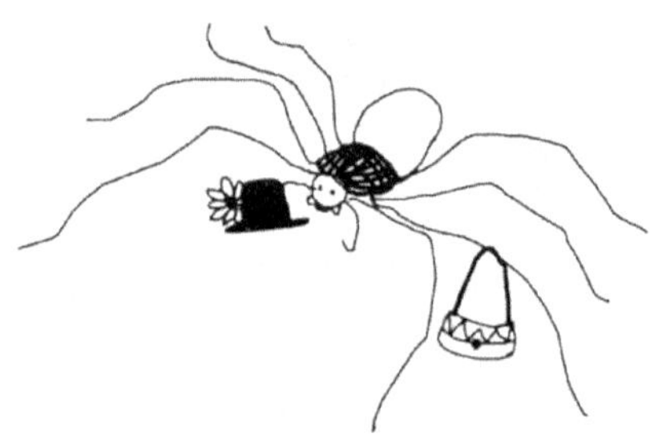

There were girls who guarded the swings during recess and after classes. They wouldn't let you play unless they thought you were cool or you were their friend.

I was too afraid to say anything, so I waited for the dragon to come pick me up. My unicorn usually came along with him and the two of us would have fun in the playground.

There were many times I wished I could stand up to those girls. Telling an adult made me worry about being called a tattletale.

I did not want to feel helpless.

Why are bullies still shielded and victims called the worst names?

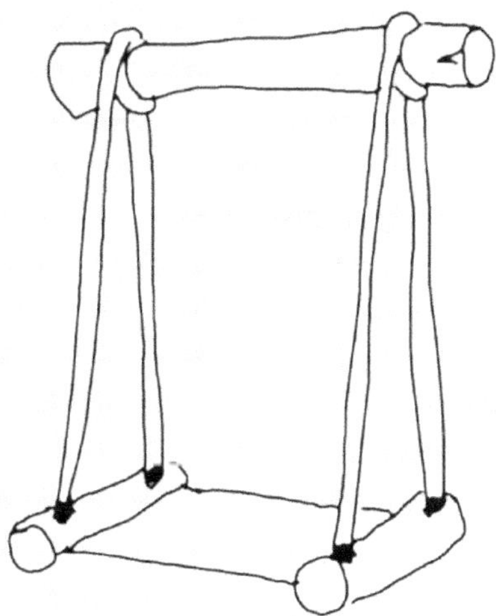

I couldn't let any of them see how afraid I was to go to school.

I was a big girl, right? The dragon and mermaid seemed to be more worried these days, plus I also knew how much my unicorn wanted to be in my shoes someday, so I waved bravely to all of them when they dropped me off at the nursery gate and smiled with great superiority at my unicorn.

Seemed right that I should set a good example, even if it meant hiding how terrified I was of getting bullied by those girls who were bigger than I was.

Learning how to stay invisible was a skill that started here

The unicorn would wait eagerly for me to return from school.

She loved the treats I would bring if there was a classmate's birthday. I would then slice my candies equally into four. The mermaid and the dragon had taught us to share what we had.

Moments like this made my unicorn impatient to start school right away and I couldn't help wanting to impress her, knowing I could succeed quite easily.

She did not know that I was being bullied by a kid who focused her temper on me.

I loved watching her eyes widen at all my made-up stories.

There was going to be trouble if anyone dared hurt my unicorn

I adored the Tamarind tree on our school campus.

Its deep roots and wide branches made it a majestic sight like as if it was proudly showing off its grandeur. The tree had a personality of its own, and cutting it down would have been a crime. Located at the end of the sports field, it was a constant presence during our Physical Education/Training (PE/PT) classes, which I disliked due to the teachers.

After learning how to write an "excuse me from the sports" letter, I'd sit on the compound's short ledge and secretly stuff fallen tamarind fruits into my skirt pocket when the Sports Master wasn't looking. Later, I'd crack open the shell and savor the juicy, slightly sour seeds. I'd bring some home for the unicorn and dolphin to enjoy until they started school and discovered the thrill themselves. Many classmates and students from other grades shared this delight, making it a forbidden yet exciting activity.

If you haven't experienced this, I suggest finding a tamarind tree to understand the thrill.

I wonder if that tree still stands as tall and as grand as in those days

Bata was our go-to shoe brand because it was economical.

Their shoes were also incredibly sturdy and long-lasting. The dragon and the mermaid always had a clever trick up their sleeve—they'd buy us shoes a size bigger than we needed, ensuring that each pair would last for three years. This meant that the unicorn and dolphin would often inherit my hand-me-down shoes until our circumstances improved.

On PE/PT days, we were required to wear white sneakers, which made us vulnerable to mischievous classmates who'd deliberately scuff or stamp on our shoes, leaving behind unsightly mud stains. But, thanks to a quick-thinking classmate, I discovered a clever hack to whiten my shoes and avoid getting into trouble—simply rub them with chalk! It was a simple yet effective solution that saved me from many a scolding.

The shoes we wear have a way of telling us who we are

Every morning before school, the mermaid would comb our hair.

Since I had longer hair, I had to braid it, while the unicorn wore two pigtails that framed her adorable face, and the dolphin wore a headband to keep her short, bouncy curls out of her sweet little face.

Once upon a time, the mermaid used to take care of her appearance, wear makeup and even add a *pottu* (bindi). But one day, she just stopped paying attention to herself, and I wasn't sure what had happened. She stopped smiling, started yelling more frequently, and lost her patience.

Somewhere along the way, the mermaid had lost her spark

I only asked for things that were absolutely necessary.

I remember telling the unicorn and dolphin not to ask the dragon to buy things because we couldn't afford it. They would listen sometimes, but they were too young to understand what I saw.

The mermaid was more practical so she'd say no right away. However, the dragon couldn't resist giving us what we asked for.

But sometimes, I know it hurt him to say no.

Keeping the ache of wanting within you in the dark
teaches you how to wait to birth dreams in the light

The dragon enjoyed recording our voices, as well as those of our visitors.

He would bring out his treasured old cassette player and record over an old tape. If the tape came loose, he would use a pencil to insert it into one of the spool holes and roll it back into place.

The dragon also had a passion for collecting coins and stamps. I vividly remember the piggy bank with a blue hat. He had an impressive collection from around the world, which he gave to the unicorn when she expressed interest in continuing it. I'm unsure why he stopped collecting stamps or if the collection was lost, leading him to abandon the hobby. One summer, he taught the unicorn and me how to remove old stamps, trace, and shade paisa coins—a fun activity.

The dragon would share stories about his father's Ambassador and how he would drive it for everyone. He loved cars and bikes, but I suspect he lacked encouragement in his creative pursuits during his youth.

Why did the dragon not believe in the legions of talent he was sitting with?

I had to go to the dentist.

So far the tooth fairy had been my favorite mystery. I had made a rupee per fallen tooth and five rupees for the bigger ones. I used to save them to buy gifts for special occasions.

When the dentist told the dragon and mermaid they weren't allowed inside, I got frightened, so when he approached me with the injection, I screamed, jumped down from the tall chair and ran out of the room looking for the dragon and mermaid.

I refused to go back.

The mermaid spanked me in frustration, the dragon threatened and coaxed, but I had turned stubborn and nothing could have induced me to go back to the dentist. I knew they were upset with me, but how could they know about the irrational fears I carried inside?

I was determined to bear the pain silently because the dragon and mermaid warned me not to cry to them if I wasn't willing to listen. It was an empty threat. The moment I had the inevitable toothache, I was given painkillers and antibiotics to soothe the inflammation.

I think everyone was relieved when the rotten tooth eventually fell off by itself.

Assumptions that I was fussing, oversensitive or reacting in an abnormal way began here. But really, could a child of my age give anyone the right words to express what was going on when I didn't know or understand it myself?

I've despised dentists ever since then.

There are those who feel the depth of the ocean
more strongly than those who walk on land

I would describe him as charming, captivating, and cunning as a fox.

Unfortunately, I did not know this cousin well, as he and his older sister were taken away from the main branch of the family when they were quite young. When he grew older, he made the first attempt to reconnect with us. I remember meeting him when I was a little girl, just back from school. He made me laugh so hard, and we played cards together, along with the dragon.

I saw him again later, this time with his sister, and I thought she was beautiful, with the most stunning dimples. Although I was more cautious this time around, I couldn't help but feel affection for them both. They would continue to appear and disappear from our lives. If only they had been brought up in our world…

She is the eldest cousin sister from the mermaid's side though that space of big sister over us went to the next two in line. We attended her wedding, and later, I met her beautiful children, who inherited her stunning looks.

I felt a deep sadness when I learned that he had passed away from a heart attack at such a young age, but that didn't happen until I was in my thirties. Time, life, and the consequences of actions had separated us, preventing a lasting bond.

Sometimes, I wished things had been different

I remember this like a distant memory that comes up to the surface; the kind you want to push back, afraid of what it meant, not sure you can handle it.

We were playing hide and seek, when the younger girl behind me pulled down my panties and kissed me there. I yelled and shoved her. She said it was a game and it was supposed to feel good. It happened several times as she tried to convince me, but I kept resisting and saying I didn't like it. She and her sister would shift uncomfortably, refuse to play, or just ignore me. Eventually, this stopped and we continued playing other games.

I didn't tell the dragon and mermaid. I didn't have the words to tell them what had been happening because I myself did not understand it. All I cared about in that moment was that I would get into big trouble and they might not let me play with those girls again.

When I began writing again after a long period, I recalled every aspect of these memories in horror as the wounds of violation and betrayal surfaced from where they had been existing in some dark corner of my heart.

When I disclosed it to my friend, she shocked me with another perspective.

How did children aged six and nine know about things that children should not?

Innocence is a wound that bleeds words it does not know

When my cousin had a baby sister, I was thrilled!

I eagerly asked to hold her, but she refused, even when I promised it would only be for a minute. My godmother, witnessing our exchange, reassured me not to worry. When I asked why, she revealed that she had a baby on the way and promised I could carry her whenever I wanted once she arrived. I looked at her barely visible bump, thinking she was just being kind, so I smiled politely, wiped away my tears and agreed with her.

I had been pestering the mermaid for another baby every day, and when I increased my begging, she would get frustrated and tell me to quiet down. I thought having a baby was easy or that we could adopt one whenever we wanted. I prayed to the Weaver to let me adopt babies one day so I could love them. At that young age, I didn't grasp the responsibilities and emotional maturity required to care for a baby, but the desire to have them was sparked in my heart.

When I first saw Ruth, the deep emotions I felt—awe, love, and happiness—overwhelmed me. "She's so small," I told my godmother when the dragon took me to visit. "And she cries like a baby sheep," I added, as she let out a soft cry. My godmother found this description entertaining and burst out laughing.

Her birth was around the time I started going for my first Holy Communion classes and because I loved her, I read about the story of *Ruth*. I already loved the Biblical stories of *Sarah, Miriam, Esther and Suzanna,* plus the saints—*Agnes* and *Maria (Goretti)*—so when the Catechism teacher asked me what names I would choose for my Confirmation, I gave her all of them.

She laughed and said I could have only one so when I pray I could request their added prayers. I didn't answer because that did not make sense to me. I already spoke to my favorite saints and asked for their help over many things so I just smiled at her. I went to the Weaver and prayed and asked if I could have all eight of them, including my middle name—*Johanna.* I didn't hear Him say no, though I did feel His amusement. Who said I couldn't have more names? I was keeping them.

Ruth was the only cousin I carried, fussed over, and babied the most. I liked to believe she was my baby. "After she grows up, will she remember that I held her like this?" I would ask my godmother and she would always tell me that Ruth would which she still does to this day.

As she grew, she disliked being in her crib for too long, so whenever she cried, I'd rush to carry her or find excuses to wake her up just to hold her.

She was my living doll and today, she is the mother of three

I remember my *First Holy Communion* vividly. The previous day I attended my first confession and experienced my first connection with the Holy Spirit.

My unicorn had done something to annoy me deliberately, but I did not get angry or upset because a voice cautioned me to choose gentleness instead. I listened and I felt a rich, bubbling sensation of joy flutter throughout my body. I felt so happy in that moment, I hugged everyone.

Of course, there were times I did not listen to this voice of truth and chose my own instead, but whenever I do listen, I feel that powerful sensation of unbridled ecstasy.

The Dove of Grace adorned my head with a crown of myrtle flowers

I knew she was amazing the day she rescued Gray's nose when it fell off. She patched him up with a big green marble and wiped away my tears. She told me that my stuffed dog had had a rough time in surgery and would need extra love and care.

I made sure that Gray went to sleep right between Snoopy (my favorite stuffed toy that the dragon and the mermaid had gifted me), Teddy, and myself for a very long time.

I loved Sabrina.

**True kindness is a rare gift to receive from anyone
and whenever I do experience it, I soak in its warmth**

I remember the sting of a teacher's slap because I didn't finish my homework.

Before I could explain, her hand made contact with my face, sending me stumbling off balance. The force of the slap left a persistent ringing in my ears for days. I wasn't the only victim; this teacher regularly slapped students, and we had all come to accept it as normal.

I assumed teachers had parental authority when the dragon and mermaid weren't around, given the era we grew up in, where teachers were always right. Fear kept me from telling the dragon and mermaid; I thought they'd side with the teacher. But when I finally shared the story with them years later, they were upset that it had happened.

My experience with some teachers were a harsh contrast to the ideal of what a teacher ought to be but I do have my favorites and they know who they are.

Teachers should be the first to embody gentleness in their hands

I must admit, I didn't enjoy my SUPW (Socially Useful Productive Work) classes as much as I should have.

Although they were supposed to be relaxing and a break from our academic routine, I remember two teachers who had a disappointing temperament. They appeared pleasant and courteous to the staff, but behind closed doors, they revealed a mean streak that I found quite off-putting. Their behavior was a stark contrast to the calm and creative atmosphere that SUPW classes were meant to foster.

When we focused on art or learning simple skills like paper crafting or painting, it was bearable. I even enjoyed our mid-year exhibition, where we showcased our creativity to the dragon and mermaid. They would marvel at our handmade projects, and we would beam with pride. One year in primary school, the dragon painted an impressive depiction of a frog's metamorphosis for me, which the biology teacher admired so much that I did not get it back! It remained on display in the lab for a while until it was taken down.

However, when it came to knitting, I hit a mental block. My friend, who was exceptionally skilled with the needles, tried to guide me patiently, but I just couldn't seem to get the hang of it. I would struggle to cast on, or my stitches would be uneven, and I would end up with a tangled mess. Thankfully, the mermaid came to my rescue, finishing my project in one sitting for the exhibition. She was also incredibly talented in embroidery, creating intricate patterns and designs with ease. Her skills were impressive, and I often found myself in awe of her creativity.

Despite the challenges and frustrations, SUPW classes taught me the value of perseverance and the importance of exploring different creative outlets. And, of course, I will always cherish the memories of my friends and family members who helped me through the tough times.

I eventually took up crocheting in my twenties and came to love it

The unicorn and I giggled, up to our usual mischief.

Banished to the bedroom while the mermaid watched her favorite shows, *Bold and Beautiful* and *Santa Barbara,* we concocted a game of sneaking peeks through the slightly ajar door. Curious about why the dragon and mermaid deemed these shows off-limits, we hid behind the door, watching as on-screen couples locked eyes for what felt like an eternity before finally sharing a kiss.

We exchanged scandalized glances, thrilled by our daring discovery. Kissing—so that was what they didn't want us to see! Giggling over our deplorable ways, we high-fived each other, feeling like we'd uncovered an adult secret.

As I drifted off to sleep, I pondered the difference between TV kisses and real-life ones. Was it something bad or just forbidden for us?

I wanted my future husband and I to be kissing like that.

How did they make everything seem so much more magical on screen?

The dragon insisted on one meal a day being eaten together as a family, plus he also had another important golden rule—"Finish everything on your plate, including your vegetables, or you can't get up from the table."

We grumbled, but obeyed with a few amendments. The unicorn disliked veggies with a passion so they somehow made their way to the dolphin's plate, which she ate quite happily—completely oblivious—much to our amusement.

But what we enjoyed the most were the games that the dragon insisted we play during meal times. Games that meant naming animals, birds, flowers, including presidents, countries and capitals, etc., which are his favorite subjects because he is a huge Geography buff; often poring over maps or dictionaries for hours on Sundays when he isn't watching his favorite Westerns or listening to Jim Reeves.

He increased our general knowledge, made us think about current events, and cultivated our minds.

The dolphin, unicorn, and the moon
had begun to dream about worlds outside their own

Reena Doss

I recall a neighbor who seemed to knit all day and had many cats who played with her yarn as if it were theirs.

Whenever she left her wool lying around, her cats would somehow get comfy between their fibrous strands. I thought it was surprising how they did not get themselves tangled, but would eye me belligerently with lazy lids, tails swaying. Was it animosity or fascination? The mermaid didn't like cats too much so I was not quite sure why I liked them, though not as much as dogs.

I liked visiting her, dubbing her *Catwoman* secretly in my head. She was kind and compassionate and craved company. I did not know the reasons why she was left alone in her delightful British cottage with her quaint little weedy garden.

I did not forget her and the cats. I think of them from time to time.

Some people create perceptions that linger throughout your life

I think she was a nun, if my memory serves me correctly.

She possessed prophetic abilities and, when praying over each of us, told me that I had the gift of love. I was perplexed, knowing it wasn't a traditional gift of the Holy Spirit, but rather an inherent aspect of the Weaver's nature, accessible to everyone. I didn't grasp her meaning, and perhaps she struggled to interpret the vision herself. Since I believed the Weaver had a purpose for me, I felt disappointed when told I was given love. I asked the Weaver if I was unsuitable for His Kingdom of service. I was upset when I thought He didn't answer me.

I confided in the unicorn and dolphin, envying their gifts of wisdom and intelligence. The unicorn said something wise: "Reena, God is love, and having love means God is love so He will always be with you." The dolphin nodded in agreement as this made logical sense to her.

Though I didn't fully understand at the time, that moment set me on my destined path. Unbeknownst to me, life was equipping me with essential tools before it would break me apart. It was a necessary process, but one I wouldn't comprehend until I was ready to release certain parts of me on my journey towards my dreams.

The Weaver answers us in many ways; we must be prepared to listen

Birthdays were simple and low-key affairs in our family.

Occasionally, the dragon, a family member, or friend would surprise us with a cake to mark the occasion. We didn't have formal birthday celebrations, but we always looked forward to seeing our cousins. With 15 cousins on the dragon's side and 15 on the mermaid's side, plus the three of us, we had a large and lively family. I was the 6th eldest on the dragon's side and the 6th youngest on the mermaid's side. Our younger cousins who lived nearby would always join us, but some cousins wouldn't attend, either due to concerns about our neighborhood or because they lived abroad.

Extended family get-togethers with the mermaid's family were rare and special occasions, filling us with excitement. In contrast, gatherings with the dragon's family were mandatory for all of us because we were all close by. While mostly enjoyable, these events could be a mixed bag. The issue wasn't that the cousins didn't get along but many of us wished the adults would let us have our own party, free from their supervision. As kids, we had created memories and didn't need the adults to shape our experiences. The adults wanted us to be part of their memories, but they didn't realize we had formed our own.

I would also take a packet of toffees or sweets to school and for one day, I would have a *Cinderella* moment. I could wear a beautiful dress that wasn't my usual uniform. I would be treated like a princess and everyone would act super nice. The class teacher would make the class sing *Happy Birthday* for me, clap for the number of years I was born plus one extra for God's love. Then the class would say "We love you, Reena." And I would say, "Thank you, my friends." It was like a choreographed script for every birthday, just like in morning assembly when we would sing our national and school anthem. I suppose here is also where I got into the habit of addressing any friend as "my friend". And though I rolled my eyes at all these routines, I secretly loved it because it was on my birthday that I got to be visible.

I wonder where some of the friends I lost touch with are;
I hope they are doing well

I hated how they treated us; like children desperate for their fine things, when all we craved was a little kindness. Sometimes their actions, though harmless to them, hurt and affected us. "Put those toys away, play with the broken ones!" or "Put them in the cupboard and lock them!"

How many times have we heard this horrible stricture aimed at their kids but still audible enough to us. Like as though their folks had already labelled as broken or feared that we would do something to their toys. What kind of mentality did you have to have to teach your own children that they were superior to others?

In truth, we were the most well-mannered and well-dressed children. The mermaid saw to that. Sometimes, the dragon would fight for us and later on, he stopped as we grew and told him not to.

These were the people who didn't seem to know that there were those who were able to buy gifts from shops and we couldn't. Yet they placed them above our handmade cards that we'd slaved over for many hours. They fell to the ground many times, uncared for, no matter how many times I bent to set them back carefully on the stand.

We knew that we were already blessed but we heard, we saw, and we felt their rejection.

Weren't we children too?

**Superficial sophistication is often a cruel excuse
to disregard the value of another person's feelings**

I delighted in crafting gifts, cards, and planning surprise gestures. The unicorn and dolphin shared my enthusiasm, also expressing their creativity in unique ways.

One time, the dolphin created a thoughtful gift during her needlework class—a piece of cloth featuring three knitted hearts. When I asked about their significance, she explained that the first heart represented me, the second symbolized the unicorn, and the third stood for herself. She added that it served as a reminder for me to cherish the love I carry. I treasure this keepsake in my memories and revisit it when needed.

Often, I incorporate three hearts into posts, letters, or messages as a tribute to the love I hold, the dolphin's thoughtfulness, and my three siblings. Sometimes, I even replace the "e" in my first name with two hearts plus an extra one, embracing the symbolism of three—reflecting the Holy Trinity (the Father, the Son and the Holy Spirit), I Corinthians 13:13 line (Hope, Faith and Love), the octopus's three hearts, and my love for creative expression.

R <3 <3 <3 n a

It was extraordinary to notice and observe the care the dragon and mermaid had for each other and us; the way darkness could not penetrate our circle of love.

They were best friends, yet it was a curious thing for me to watch them struggle with their insecurities and worries on a daily basis. They did not lose faith in the Weaver's providence no matter what and they somehow worked things out together.

It was this touching vulnerability that made me think about how I would like that someday too.

Marriage is a sacred sacrament that only the Weaver can anoint and bless

I loved when the dragon would stop the bike to buy fresh coconuts from a street vendor on the way home from school. I enjoyed watching the vendor hack the shell open, stick a straw in, and give it to us to drink.

Did you know that these vendors are the ones who climb a coconut tree with just their feet and a rope? The amount of coconuts they manage to bring down is literally their livelihood for the day. So always get one if you can. It helps them.

I know many people won't get it, but have you ever tasted fresh coconut water and eaten its succulent, soft flesh? It's a delicacy here in the Summer and extremely good for health.

I loved those rare times when the dragon would buy them for us.

**The softness of the coconut is its true nature
once you get past its hard exterior**

I remember us on that Silver Plus bike, heading home after visiting Grandy. We slipped and fell into the ditch. The dragon and the mermaid got hurt, the dolphin had fallen flat on her face despite the mermaid trying to shield her, and the unicorn by some stroke of luck had jumped off and remained unscathed. I was bleeding from the corner of my eye. The mermaid was scared that I had hurt my eye and had been blinded but she laughed tenderly when I told her tearfully that I wished I had been the only one who had got hurt, not them.

Cars passed us by in a hurry, all except one. I'll always remember their kindness. They were dressed well, probably going for an important function, but they still stopped and took the mermaid and us to the hospital. The dragon came later. The dragon, the mermaid and I only sustained surface wounds that would eventually fade away. However, it was our baby dolphin who had to receive stitches on her forehead which would leave behind a permanent little scar.

The man in the car found Teddy at the scene of the accident and brought him to me. I couldn't tell him how much that mattered and gave him the biggest smile I could summon. I thought my heart was going to burst with happiness and relief.

The amusing aspect of this miserable night was the nurse who kept chasing my unicorn around the hospital bed even though she was the only one who didn't get a scratch.

I laughed so hard because I knew no one could catch her. She was way too fast. The mermaid finally yelled at the nurse to stop chasing her. When the nurse halted in her tracks, the unicorn looked at me and grinned.

It wasn't such a bad day after all.

The Sun is present even in the direst situations

The mermaid was holding the unicorn in her arms on the top step of a street shop. The dragon was talking to the shopkeeper and I was looking at the glass display.

Suddenly, I heard a scream. The mermaid was on the floor, yelling in pain. When she started crying, the unicorn and I also began crying.

The dragon was on the floor beside the mermaid, men racing toward the shop's shelter, the dragon carrying the mermaid, the mermaid leaving in a car, the unicorn holding my hand tightly…

I saw all this in a flash like I was out of my body. Numbness took over as I stared at everything, feeling detached. I didn't realize I had begun doing this whenever I felt helpless.

When the mermaid came back from the hospital, her leg was in a cast. The dragon told us later that the mermaid had slipped on the top stair and fractured her leg.

Despite her crutches, she would still handwash our clothes and cook our meals. I remember the dragon putting me in charge of the unicorn so he could help her with the things she couldn't do.

Life started picking up the pace and setting adversity on us.

The unexpected will happen, but if you have a good team, you can paddle through the storm even if you are in a little boat

One afternoon, our teachers surprised us by screening *Home Alone-1* in the classroom, a lucky treat since our main teachers were absent.

This film, along with its sequel, remains a favorite of mine. I deeply connected with the protagonist, Kevin, who embodied a relatable mix of innocence, mischief, and feelings of invisibility. Despite being told he was loved, Kevin felt unseen, a sentiment that resonated with me. This connection helped me navigate the complex emotion of feeling invisible. In fact, it has helped me to achieve things others thought would be impossible for me to do.

When the movie aired on our cable, I re-watched it with my family, and it was even more enjoyable. The mermaid identified with the mother's character, while the dragon memorized lines from the bumbling burglars, using them to make us laugh. The unicorn, dolphin, and I imagined ourselves as Kevin's co-conspirators.

It was the first movie that made me feel like I was in a theater

I asked my aunt if I could have one more slice of cake. It was chocolate caramel with fresh cream oozing down its sides.

She said no in a way that made my eyes water. I was only five and I didn't understand why this wasn't possible when other little hands were given what I'd asked for.

There was still so much more leftover to give.

Please, may I have one more?

Little World

I had already begun to feel
the sting of life's true nature—
C H A N G E…

It was uncomfortable
I wanted to be protected
yet I wanted to be strong enough
so that it would not be necessary

I knew I wanted to explore the outside
but it was frustrating
waiting on time
to grow me up
to adulthood

I sat in my little world
wondering what lay beyond

I wanted to see everything
but I was still acquiring
a unique surface coating

shell

of a Pearl

II
SHELTERED

The notion of feeling sheltered is at best an illusion;
a soft blanket we wear to protect us from the cold reality.

Pillars

As I learned
about life's lessons
I discovered an eternal sky of shelter
structured and maintained by those I loved
keeping me safe and warm through the toughest times
even as I realized no one under it could be protected indefinitely
because life's important battles had to be faced
alone.
This was the first and permanent lesson
I learned

temporary

at home

I thought she was joking at first.

"It's nothing personal, but if you did well, my parents would let me hang out with you". The girl who was supposed to be a friend told me that quite frankly. I used to get invited to her birthday parties, but how quickly she changed her tune when she found I was useless to her.

A few high-ranking students didn't like to hang out with those who didn't do as well as them for fear of contracting the supposed "failing disease".

This odd idea of excellence surprised me. I had often found many of my classmates—who had failed consistently in all their papers—to be far more intelligent than the ones who scored distinctions by memorizing textbooks.

The dragon and mermaid had taught me that being kind was more important and I'm so glad that I listened.

Success is a lonely place to be when no one is standing with you

I had a fight with my cousin that day. We were all there together upstairs, children playing in that room away from the adults.

They trusted him. He was young, polite and not exactly an immediate uncle, more like an extended relative who would lurk around at our gatherings. We called him Uncle.

I was six, I think, or less when he spotted me sitting away from the rest, alone and upset; the perfect candidate.

"Why aren't they playing with you?" he asked, in such a caring voice.

Child that I was, I told him that they didn't want to be my friend. He promised he would be my friend. He pulled me onto his lap and then slowly, almost gently, started to rub my body from my chest to the V between my skinny legs that dangled way above the ground. I tried to get off, but he told me we wouldn't be friends anymore if I did.

That bothered me because I liked him and he was being so kind, right? Maybe I was a bad person. I grew uncomfortable, I didn't understand. I didn't have names for what he was doing.

Someone called him and he ran downstairs. I remember trying to drag the unicorn away from the others, but she wanted to stay. I ran downstairs just as he was coming up and he tried to block me, telling me I couldn't come up if I chose to go downstairs. He picked me up, but I struggled and kicked him. It surprised him and he put me down, calling me a crybaby.

The mermaid came running, carrying the dolphin. I said my stomach was paining and could we please leave because I felt sick. She looked relieved—and so did he— that that was all I had to say and my supposed Uncle left to go upstairs.

The mermaid told me to go tell the unicorn to get ready.

He had put on some fancy music and was treating them all like mini-adults. I couldn't explain why that felt off. Luckily, the dragon came to get her and that disgusting man couldn't say or do anything more damaging.

When I didn't stop crying even after going home, the mermaid knew something was terribly wrong. She asked me what happened upstairs and made me narrate it, giving me her hand to get me to show her. I still remember her look of horror as she looked at the dragon. They were infuriated, but they didn't know what action to take. They wanted to do something, but it was hard to do anything in a society that did not care unless you were raped, where people judge the child molested, rather than the molester. They opted instead to keep a distance from him and told me to tell them if anyone did that again.

They let me stay home the next day. No school, I was glad. I started having the falling dream soon after.

My supposed Uncle didn't take my clothes off, but he rubbed my body. I was not grown up. He shouldn't have.

What pleasure did he get from it? I wondered as a grown-up, feeling sick as I relived this memory.

Photographic memories stayed with me. Heavy metal loudly blaring, closed-off small room, smell of cheap beer on his breath.

I hate heavy metal, closed spaces, and the smell of that particular beer.

Those who choose not to drink should not be judged too quickly

I was afraid to speak up because the teacher was known to be very strict.

I finally summoned up the courage to ask permission to use the restroom, but she insisted I hold it in. I told her it was urgent, but she yelled at me to go sit in my seat.

When I peed in my uniform, the girl next to me shrieked and the teacher dragged me out of my seat and screamed at me in front of my class.

I started crying when they laughed. I was sent to get changed but then I had to come back and mop up my mess. This was the teacher's method to prevent anything like that from happening again.

I didn't know how to tell the dragon and mermaid about it so I made up a story about another girl who went through what I did.

I felt better.

Children should feel safe in the hands of those they are entrusted to

I remember not completing my homework. I was shaking when I went up to tell the teacher, knowing what was coming, but still not expecting the sting of tears and the sudden shock of feeling deaf temporarily when her cruel hand left fingerprints on my cheek.

What was the point of bothering the mermaid and the dragon about this when I hadn't done my homework in the first place?

I didn't say anything.

Fear is rancid food fed in intervals

The dragon liked to smoke.

This habit worried me when I learned to read the warning labels on his *Wills* or *Gold Flakes* packs: "Injurious to health". I confided in the unicorn, and we decided to take action, especially after being exposed to awareness programs at school. The unicorn came up with a plan to secretly dispose of a few cigarettes at a time.

Initially, the dragon didn't notice, but when he did, we knew we were in trouble. Fortunately, the dragon was more amused than irritated by our actions and sternly told us not to repeat them. However, the turning point came when we brought home cigarette candies and pretended to smoke them.

That's when he finally quit.

Transformation doesn't rely on perfect timing; it happens when one is ready, or not at all

The three of us were by default little Raggedy Anns, so getting someone else's hand-me-downs came with the territory. Unless a child or an adult said something that made us conscious about our financial situation, we did not care too much because it usually felt like Christmas morning when we got "new" stuff to wear. Occasionally, of course, we would get beautiful new clothes from some of our sweetest aunts.

The mermaid is the finest needlewoman I know and I'm certain she could have done well in the fashion industry. She and the dragon often saved up to buy pretty fabrics so she could stitch us new clothes.

Wherever we went, we knew we were undeniably well-dressed. Everyone often wanted to know where we bought our clothes from and we would proudly say, "Mama made them!"

She would slave over the sewing machine, way past midnight, bringing our ideas of fashion to life in record time, often neglecting her own needs for ours.

I thought she was a magician.

The mermaid's hands wove love into every little thing

"She's not fair enough to be considered pretty." I heard this one day as a child and for many years I suffered internally; thinking I was not beautiful, wishing I was like those pretty girls with ivory skin and rosy apple cheeks.

I was even prejudiced against those who shared my skin tones, feeling like we stood no chance against the others. I did not realize until I had grown up that we were all beautiful, and that our skin tones reflected the way the Earth looks after its first kiss under Monsoon's umbrella of rain.

Then there were others who were equally beautiful...
some kissed by Summer's light,
some by Autumn's hues,
some by Winter's snow,
and some by Spring's roses.

My eyes had opened.

**We are all so achingly beautiful like a garden
lit under the Sun's celestial sky**

She taught me how to cry by staring at the wall without blinking.

It would have been a great skill to learn whenever we got into scrapes with the dragon and mermaid, but I would start giggling—much to her frustration—and then we'd both end up laughing together at our failed attempts.

Back then, I knew there was no one else I could trust to keep my secrets. She was the one person I knew who saw things and people as they were and accepted them regardless of their history.

She was incredibly perceptive and capable of analyzing a situation objectively.

She was willing to keep her heart open.

She was dauntless.

Contradictions of the human heart
are beautiful things to witness when they evolve within

She struggled with her speech and it wasn't because she was nervous or shy.

In fact, she was bolder than anyone I knew. She didn't hesitate to speak up when it was necessary to ask for what she needed. One day, she turned it into her strength: she used it to slip with perfect ease into speaking the romantic languages. Then she took this skill to another level and turned it into an art form that distinguishes her from the rest.

I admire her because even when people were not understanding, she never let it bother her. I hope she always remembers to come back to herself.

She was kind to those who were unkind.

She was thoughtful toward those who were thoughtless.

She was determined in the face of failure.

True bravery is the act of turning your weakness into a strength that serves humanity

As the three of us grew, we discovered our own unique personalities.

My unicorn and I had to choose opposing sides of the coin. It was a given. We had to disagree on everything, but it had its purpose, as we learned who we were and what we stood for.

Our dolphin always chose the winning side, but it was not a fun day for her if we ganged up on her.

Sibling warfare can teach you much about conflict resolution and communication

The mermaid and the dragon used to hug us when we were children.

I did not realize that they were not naturally demonstrative until I grew up and craved this affection from them as a teenager and adult. I suppose it was easier for them when we were kids. I know they love it when we do hug them now.

At the time, I was getting more independent and so I stopped hugging them because I wanted to act grown up.

But then, they stopped too.

Affection is a long hug wrapped up in layers of comfort, peace, and joy

One of my favorite childhood TV shows was *The Elephant Show.*

I cherished every episode, but it was a challenge to get my Grandy in a good mood to let us watch it. The theme songs were catchy, and the dragon would sing them to us, making it even more special.

The movie that captured my imagination, feelings and heart was *The Sound of Music* and which I remember with a lot of mixed emotions. My Grandy had a tape, but she'd only let us watch it when her daughter's children were around, openly showing favoritism. I remember the dragon begging her to let us see it. We finally watched it once when two Italian guests were staying at my grandmother's while she was away for the evening. One of them was called Peppino.

Peppino was friends with the mermaid from her catechist days and was delighted to meet us. His warm demeanor, gruff laugh, and white beard was exactly how I imagined Heidi's grandfather would look. I was certain the sparrows outside would be quite happy to nest in his beard. When he affectionately called me *bambino,* which meant *little child* in Italian, I thought he meant *Bambi,* like the fawn in the Disney film.

Kindness leaves a lasting impression, no matter how small the act

Building tents was a delightful adventure.

We would ask the mermaid for permission to use the clothespins, as she was quite possessive of them, relying on them to dry our clothes on the line. In those days, the mermaid didn't have the luxury of a washing machine, so she would painstakingly handwash every garment, including the dragon's, on the large stone slab that came with the rented house.

After promising to return the clips, the unicorn and I would excitedly pull out clean bedsheets from the cupboards and carefully position the chairs to mark the perimeter of our makeshift tent. With the dolphin's help, we'd spend hours clipping the sheets together, debating the perfect height and size of our structure. Meanwhile, the dolphin would often wander off to play with her dolls underneath the tent, adding to the chaos and joy of our creative endeavors.

The process of building our tent houses were often more enjoyable than the final product itself. The unicorn and dolphin loved it when I read them stories or played "house-house" with them, pretending we had to sleep under the open sky. Our imaginations ran wild, and we reveled in the freedom and adventure of our make-believe world. Those carefree moments, surrounded by the people and things I loved, are etched in my memory forever.

Why do we lose the desire to dream up such imaginative adventures as adults?

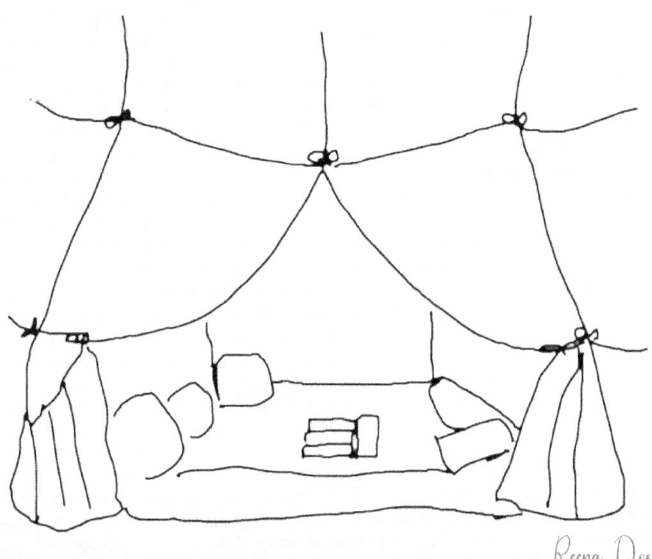

I fondly remember watching *Captain Planet* with the unicorn and dolphin.

As environmental science students, we were captivated by the show's creative use of elements to form a superhero, *Captain Planet,* and its mission to raise environmental awareness. The diverse backgrounds of the teenage characters, all passionate about preserving nature, resonated with us. I was entranced by the idea of becoming planeteers, united to protect the Earth by using the elements.

The unicorn, dolphin, and I would enthusiastically sing the theme song, belting out "Earth, Fire, Wind, Water, Air..." and eagerly await *Captain Planet's* introduction and continue on with singing, "Looting and polluting is not the way…" After he would emphasize that the power lies within us to make a difference, we'd excitedly join in, reciting the phrase "...saving our planet is the thing to do!" We knew the entire song by heart and we would sing it with gusto.

I wish the new generation could experience the show's impact, as it certainly left a lasting impression on us.

The power to make a difference indeed lies within us

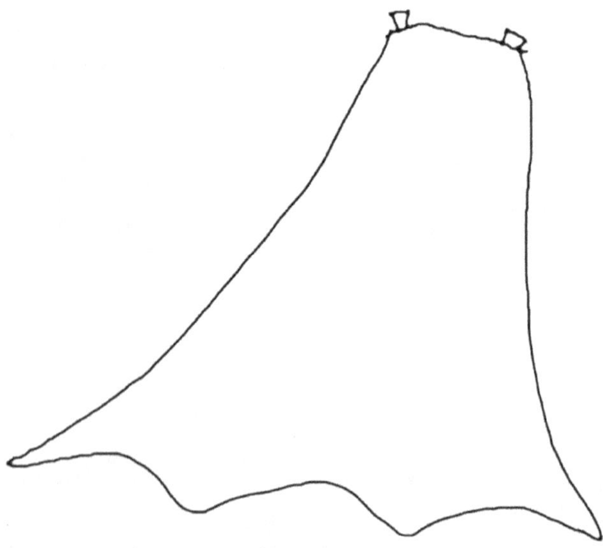

I remember feeling happy about moving to Calcutta. It didn't seem bad in the wake of all that I had seen so far.

The dragon was cheated out of his shop and he lost a lot, but he refused to fight for what he considered material things. He was full of integrity and upheld traditional codes of honor that weren't acceptable assets in the business world of sharks.

The mermaid was still recovering from her broken leg and she had no time to be sad because we needed her.

It was the end of the monsoons when we packed up and headed to the mermaid's and my birthplace, excited to meet my uncle and his family there.

I wanted a new start and so did my family.

Endings open up opportunities for growth and restoration

I liked the mermaid's brother so very much. He was extremely intelligent and though he could be intimidating to talk to at first, I later discovered that his heart was pure gold and he often saw what was left unsaid.

My aunt was not demonstrative, but she was one of the most thoughtful people I knew. My cousins were a lot older, but they still tried to play games and teach us things.

I fondly remember them teaching us "ant races with our toy teacups", letting us play with their dolls, making "cloth" boats for us, and letting us watch their favorite movies from their treasured collection.

They were so generous and kind.

So many leaves on a branch, so many branches attached to the trunk,
but they all belong to the tree who serves the Sun

The mermaid and the dragon were teachers now and they got extremely busy in their new roles of teaching English and Mathematics as well as trying to adapt to a new city.

I disliked the fact that I now had to learn Hindi as my second language when I had only studied Kannada so far.

I loved the attic, but was dismayed to find that this secret room housed mice. Gone were my dreams of creating a private alcove for reading there. The dragon managed to chase them away, but found a nest of new born mice. I wanted to keep them, but before I could ask, the dragon put them out in the sun to let nature take its course.

I watched in horror as birds began to circle overhead and Death came calling. It was a devastating moment when a bird grabbed a baby mouse, presumably to feed its own, and I ran inside, eyes watering.

I was too soft.

Even though nature can be an unscrupulous teacher,
it is wiser to accept her rules whenever possible

I became a bit of a bully in school because I felt the dragon and mermaid being teachers entitled me in some way. Since my classmates also liked me, I had grown rather vain. I remember the exact day when I saw the error of my ways.

It was my birthday. I had turned eight. Two girls didn't wish me and I was rude to them. They were hurt and told my class teacher who corrected me at once. When I explained my hurt feelings, she told me, "Not everyone is going to like you, but you must still be kind. Besides, just because someone acts like they can't be bothered, it doesn't mean they don't care. Perhaps, they just don't know how to show it".

I was stunned at her explanation. Ashamed of myself, I apologized quickly. The girls were surprised, but gladly accepted my apology. I made a promise to myself to always choose to be kind even when it was difficult to do so.

I will not forget that teacher for her tough love.

Teachers water our seeds and prepare us
to embrace whatever we were created to become

We slept on mattresses in the room that was for every requirement except the kitchen and bathroom. It was our bedroom, hall, TV space, and where we did our homework. If you lived in my head at this time, you would think you were inside an adventure.

When I was fast asleep one night, I dreamed that a crocodile was approaching me. Its jaws looked treacherous, and I froze. I remember turning to run at the last moment, and though I somehow escaped it, my heart was beating extra fast at witnessing this. I hoped the mermaid would believe me when I told her. I found my home and looked around for the mermaid.

I was scared when I saw her rolling on the ground like she had been hurt in her stomach. Had the crocodile got her? I started crying. I was terrified of losing her, and I went to turn her towards me so I could see and fix the cut, but there was no blood.

Surprised, I touched her, trying to understand how she appeared alive when she was dying. She told me that she was okay, but something yellow started surrounding me, not red as I had expected. That meant she wasn't dying, right?

Puzzled, I reached out to touch it and noticed that my hands were shaking. I brought the substance closer to examine it even as I tried to understand what was happening. It was then that I noticed she had disappeared, and the yellow was coming out of me. It was so bright, it blinded me. It spread widely, like as though they were under a blue sky of light. I woke up then. I was frightened. I could feel the wetness on my cheeks.

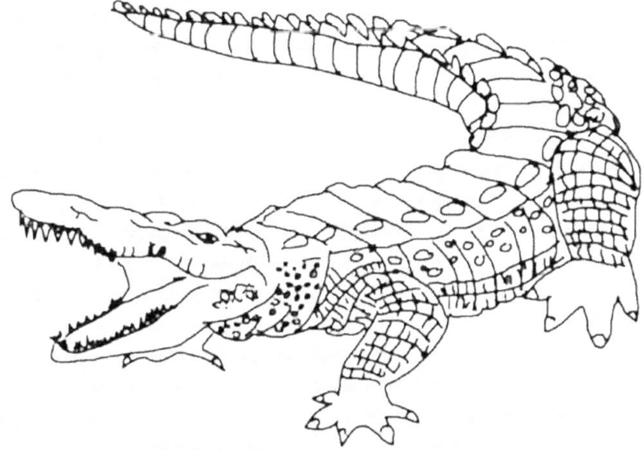

I told the mermaid parts of it because she didn't look pleased when I began to tell her.

Later on in school, when we were taught the song *Like A Sunflower,* I understood that it was sunflowers that I had seen, but the reason they confused me was because they were hazy in my dreams. They appeared almost like liquid, as if they had been soaked in water.

Yellow hands, yellow mane with a palm full of the colors of the soil, I think maybe a sunflower is a reminder of God's grace.

Dreams that we remember can sometimes hold a pathway

As a child, I adored picture books, pouring over every image and finding meaning in each detail.

Illustrations sparked my imagination, transporting me to faraway lands with the characters. My early favorites were Hans Christian Andersen's fairytales, followed by *The Grimm's* fairytales (Nutty Poopoo got us this book), and later, Enid Blyton's captivating worlds, including *Noddy, Mallory Towers, The Secret Seven, The Famous Five, Amelia Jane, The Wishing Chair,* and *The Farm* series.

When the newspapers arrived—either *The Times Of India* or *The Deccan Herald*—we would immediately turn to the movie schedule. The dragon and the mermaid would squabble over who got to do the crossword or correctly guess certain words. I, on the other hand, loved reading the comics section. *Hägar the Horrible, Moose Miller,* and *Calvin and Hobbes* were some of my absolute favorites. I would spend time poring over the colorful panels, laughing at the witty humor and clever creativity. The newspaper was a treasured part of our daily routine, bringing us together in a shared experience of entertainment and enjoyment. Later on, I moved on to the *Tinkle Comics,* which were passed around in school. Shikari Shambu, Tantri the Mantri, Suppandi, and Nasruddin Hodja were some of my favorites. Next, I indulged in Archies and Superhero comics—*Tarzan, Superman, Batman, Spiderman, Phantom,* and *Zorro* consumed my time during breaks between school and waiting to go home. I also started reading classics like *Jane Eyre, Wuthering Heights,* and *Pride and Prejudice. King Arthur, Tarzan, Robin Hood,* and *Shakespeare* were, of course, my all-time favorites.

I wasn't allowed to read Sydney Sheldon, Victoria Holt, or Mills and Boons until college, but I secretly read one M&B in my 10th year. I got into trouble for it, but it was worth the risk. The kiss and "I love you" between the hero and heroine, Laird and Anna, at the end of *Whirlwind* by Charlotte Lamb made my heart flutter. Soon after, I wanted to be called Johanna or Anna for short.

I didn't want to be Reena anymore

The dragon brought home a stack of books he'd found being given away during the summer. Among them, I discovered a treasure trove of amazing books with pictures, including *Heidi, The Panchatantra Tales,* and *St. Joan Of Arc.* I spent many pleasurable hours immersing myself in these stories.

Heidi's tales of living in the mountains, befriending Peter and goats, and Grandfather's beard captivated me and I spent countless hours immersed in the wonder of these pages, touching the paintings of fir trees behind the cottage and pretending I was living atop with Heidi. I envisioned myself exploring the picturesque landscape, meeting Peter, and having goats as dear friends.

The charming scenes sparked my imagination, and I reveled in the simple joys of a carefree life amidst nature's splendor. I was particularly fascinated by Grandfather's iconic snow-white mustache, which I thought added to his endearing and wise demeanor. I would entertain myself by imagining the sound of his gruff voice, puffing from a pipe at the same time, adding to the charm of his character. Those moments of creative play allowed me to escape into a world of wonder, where the beauty of the Swiss Alps and the warmth of Heidi's story came alive in my heart.

The Panchatantra was the gateway to understanding my Indian cultural roots. It introduced me to the rich heritage of our native land. Through its stories, I discovered the vibrant voices of our ancestors, who wove tales that reflected their deep connection with nature and the world around them. *The Panchatantra's* stories, belief systems, and use of the wild to convey valuable life lessons, resonated deeply with me.

One story that has stayed with me forever is the tale of the monkey and the crocodile. This story holds a special place in my heart because, before we moved to Calcutta, the dragon would regale the unicorn, dolphin and I with stories every night before bed. I would always request the monkey and crocodile story, and each time, the dragon would narrate it with such passion and creativity that it felt like I was hearing it for the first time. He had a remarkable talent for reinventing the story, adding new twists and turns that kept us enthralled. His storytelling prowess was akin to a one-man Broadway show, where he played all the characters with remarkable flair. The dragon's renditions of the monkey and crocodile story are etched in my memory, a testament to the power of storytelling and the special bond we shared.

St. Joan of Arc's story fascinated me, and I found myself deeply invested in the mystery of her history. I marveled at the courage of a 17-year-old girl, with no military background, who dared to walk into the highest court and declare her mission. Her strength, devotion, and unwavering commitment to her calling, even in the face of false persecution and ridicule, left me in awe. The fact that she was dismissed and trivialized because of her youth and gender, and forced to wear men's clothes to be taken seriously, only added to her remarkable story.

Joan's intelligent actions, honor, dignity, and grace, despite being tormented and terrorized into denying her purpose, made a profound impact on me. At the time, I didn't realize how deeply she had touched my heart. Her bravery and selflessness—as a symbol of valor, defense, and protection for France during a time of war—resonated deeply. I was thrilled to discover that her name shared a connection with my middle name, and later, when I learned of my French roots through the mermaid's side, I felt an even stronger bond to my name, heritage, and to Joan herself.

She is my favorite saint because her story had unknowingly become a part of me, and I felt a sense of pride and connection to her courage and legacy.

Little stories become the tributaries that fill the canvas of our lives

Reena Doss

I did not meet my grandfathers on both sides though I'd heard they were absolutely wonderful. My maternal Gramps died way before the mermaid got married and my paternal Grandad died after I was a year old. Apparently, he would enjoy watching me crawl and move around and let my Grandy know where I was going.

My roots were an interesting combination of facts, myths, and legends—Indian royalty, France, and warrior blood from the army.

I used to get afraid of Grandy when I was a child, but I became very fond of her from my teen years onward.

I loved Nana though, with her big beautiful eyes and kind, compassionate ways. She read stories to us and took great enjoyment in our excitement. She didn't differentiate between her grandchildren and if she had favorites, we could not tell. I felt loved in her company and I knew that she appreciated me.

When I cheekily asked about her false teeth and where they usually disappeared to (my cousin set me up for this task), she told me that the squirrels borrowed them for a bit but would return them in the morning. I was duly impressed and privately thought Nana was a secret fairy, despite my cousin showing me where she normally kept her dentures.

I loved Nana.

**Grandmothers are golden threads that twist
and restructure the other colors in the tapestry**

I vaguely recall visiting a circus in Calcutta, but some parts remain etched in my memory.

The experience was exciting, with stalls offering games, creative innovations, and people in colorful costumes before the main event. Inside the tent, I enjoyed funny clown acts, trapeze artists gliding through the air, musical performances, and animal shows where creatures seemed to move comfortably with their trainers.

However, my wonder turned to anger when I saw the whip used to control the animals. It slid past with lightning speed, inches from their bodies, if they hesitated. I watched in discomfort as a lion was made to sit on a narrow chair, with a ring of fire held in front of him. His roar of rage echoed in my heart as he jumped through the flames, only to be threatened by an electric prod when he tried to pounce on his trainer. I stopped clapping along with the audience, feeling a sense of unease. I wondered why no one was stopping this.

I turned to the mermaid and whispered, "The lion looks like it's going to bite the man." She replied, "Good, I hope it does. It's cruel to keep them in cages." I agreed, feeling relieved that she shared my concern. The rest of the performance lost its appeal for me. I yearned to free the animals but knew it was impossible. Instead, I said a silent prayer, hoping that circuses would no longer be allowed to keep wild animals captive.

Why do we harm and confine the very creatures entrusted to our care?

Reena Doss

The Zoo in Calcutta was the most exciting place for a child and it certainly was for us. The unicorn and dolphin and I loved visiting it. I think all the big cats thought my dolphin would be their next meal because they would constantly be eyeing her no matter where we moved.

I had a special fondness for *Dumbo,* the baby elephant, even getting a chance to feed him a banana once. I'd love to believe he remembered me as a full-grown adult, but though he tapped my head when I visited later, I doubt if he truly did.

I like telling everyone that he did remember me.

Am I forgettable? I don't want to be

The trains in Calcutta were the epitome of childish adventures; especially for my seven year old head that was filled with wacky, imaginative worlds.

I loved trains, but didn't fancy spending too much time in one, so the tram was the next best thing to have make-believe adventures in.

Whenever a plane would fly low, the unicorn, dolphin and I would look up and wave, quite fascinated. We dreamed about the possibilities of one day being inside one of them.

That was the height of impossible for us, so of course, we dreamed and prayed.

**The Weaver lets us dream big so He can give us
only good things in His perfect time**

I remember a boy with his glasses on a string, just so they wouldn't fall off his head and break.

"I'm clumsy", he told me, shrugging, when I asked about it. "I keep running into things". It made me smile because it wasn't so odd to me. He didn't have any parents so his grandfather was his whole world.

"I like kids", he blurted out randomly, when I introduced him to the unicorn and dolphin. "Do you like them too?" he asked.

"Yes", I said, "I'd like to have 26 kids so that all their names can start with each letter of the alphabet".

His eyes got very wide and his jaw dropped. Then he chuckled and asked, "Maybe we should get married then?"

I agreed. He gave me a Perk bar from his bag and held my hand.

I felt extremely grown up.

It was my first proposal.

The many maybes are a casket of funeral flowers

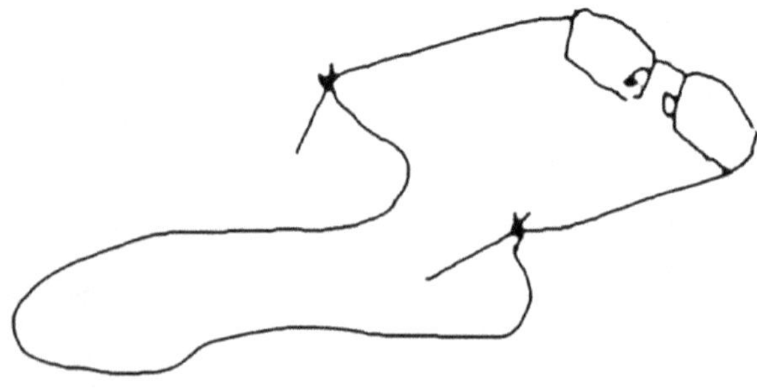

The dragon sat us down one evening and spoke to us about the Weaver, the matchmaker. I will not forget what he said. I thought about it the whole day and on my pillow at night.

I could not believe that the Weaver had created someone special for me, planned from the beginning of all eternity, much before He created this world. I couldn't grasp such brilliance, but I knew even at such an early age that that was some powerful magic.

I cherished this promise for my future and kept it close to my heart.

I am glad I let those words influence my tomorrows.

The One is real, though I wonder how long I would have to wait to meet him

I liked imitating the dragon and the mermaid when they would sing to us. When I was allowed to hold a pencil or a crayon, I would scribble on anything I could find until I was told I couldn't use the wall as my blank canvas.

I was very influenced by my talented and artistic dragon, even though he did not think he was good enough to get noticed as a professional. The mermaid didn't understand why I kept sketching people. She tried to encourage me to try something else, but I stubbornly refused to do so.

However, my unicorn and dolphin loved my art because I would tell them stories with it. I recall many days sitting by candlelight or during a rainy day, painting, sketching or singing to them.

I later realized that the reason I loved sketching people more than anything else was because they fascinated me. I especially loved drawing their eyes because it felt like they were alive. I've often thought that eyes can say a lot more than the words that come out of a mouth.

I was able to sense people's feelings and perceive things about them that they did not need to say out loud. It was a gift, but if I had to share that with anyone…

Well, I'll leave that to your imagination.

Some things are inexplicable, but I knew the Weaver had a purpose for the gift He'd given me

The mermaid's sibling's kids were the closest in age to us from the others so we often had more common ground to bond over.

My older cousin enjoyed planning fun things for us to do. She would make us dress up and perform fashion shows. I looked up to her a lot.

My cousin brother and I would tell each other our secrets, talk about serious stuff that only 7-year-olds could have, and act goofy when we played board games.

My younger cousin would listen for hours to our stories and then pepper us with a zillion-and-one questions.

We had a huge get-together with almost all of the cousins from the mermaid's side at their house. It was wonderful. When the adults had left with the younger ones, my older cousins let my cousin brother and I watch *Jurassic Park* with them. We felt very grown up and included. It was a rare moment in time and I remember feeling happy. It was a sad day when we said goodbye, all of us knowing we wouldn't see them for a very, very long time.

They were flying off with the migrating birds of Summer and where they were going seemed so far away.

Great things are cemented by the Weaver
through small and big events for your dazzling future

The dragon got a good job offer, but it meant leaving us and going off to Kalimpong. In his absence, the mermaid felt a bit easier knowing her brother was close by in case there was an emergency.

The day he left, we prayed together. Six months felt like a long, long time away from all of us. I cried, the dolphin cried, even the mermaid teared up, except for the unicorn who was doing what the dragon was doing—trying to act like nothing was wrong, laughing and joking as usual. The gate closed firmly and we waved till we couldn't see him anymore.

The mermaid began to usher us into the house. That was when we noticed something was off with the unicorn.

She said she'd hurt her leg when the mermaid asked her what was wrong. The mermaid picked her up and the unicorn threw her arms around her neck tightly. Moments later, she burst out crying and just wouldn't stop. I shrugged my shoulders in confusion but to my amazement, the mermaid started laughing.

I lifted the dolphin onto my hip as I followed them inside. I felt her soft, chubby arms hug me back and I felt oddly comforted.

**Separations are tough, but it's bearable
when you know you still have each other**

The mermaid had a beautiful letter chest.

It always seemed like a treasure trove of vintage magic to me. It was filled with onion paper, writing parchments, pens, and other writing essentials.

When there were letters to be sent, the mermaid would write and stamp them, and the dragon would drop them off at the red letter box down the lane. Since he was not there to post our letters, I am guessing the mermaid's friend or brother helped with this. Occasionally, she would let us lick the envelope's adhesive strip, and we would marvel at how it seemed to seal magically before our eyes.

What is it about seeing a handwritten note that is just for you?

We were either writing or discussing amongst ourselves what to put into our letters to the dragon.

Every day, the unicorn, dolphin and I would be on the lookout for the mailman. We couldn't wait to read the dragon's replies to us.

We would also send him our stellar art because he would appreciate and comment on them in his letters to us. In retrospect though, I have no clue why we imagined we were mini Picassos.

The mermaid would get dreamy-eyed though she swore she was not the romantic type, but we knew that inside the mermaid beat the kindest heart we'd ever known.

Letters are timeless expressions of love; I hope this world does not run out of them

The mermaid showed me the enchanting art of pressing flowers between the pages of a book.

She showed me how to gently place a delicate bloom between two sheets of paper, and then carefully close the book, allowing the flower to flatten and dry. I was fascinated by this process and eagerly tried it myself, hoping to preserve the beauty of the flowers. However, my excitement got the better of me, and I found myself opening the book every day to check on the flower's progress. Unfortunately, this only led to disappointment, as the fragile petals would crumble and break apart. It wasn't until later that I realized my mistake—I should have left the flowers undisturbed, allowing them to fully dry.

At first I wished I had been more patient because then I would have been rewarded with a beautifully preserved flower until I understood the deeper lesson I was being taught by the Weaver. While preserved flowers might be a delicate keepsake to treasure, especially when given by a loved one, flowers are far more beautiful when they are free to grow, bloom and wilt as they choose.

When I receive a flower from love, that will be a first to preserve

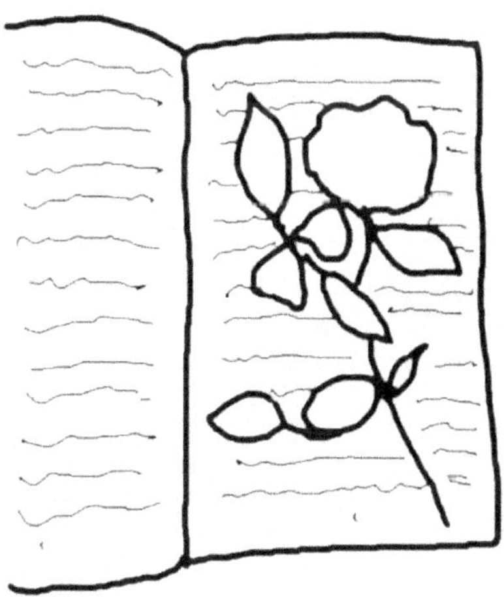

I heard the mermaid cry and it broke my heart.

I wanted to help her, but I knew I was only a child and she hid her tears from us. She missed the dragon and we didn't have our own landline. Cell phones had not made an entrance as yet. I did not like that we had to depend on others.

I would have gotten the mermaid ten phones if I could so she wouldn't miss the dragon's call.

The mermaid said I had healing hands like the dragon. She said that whenever I would offer to give her or the dragon a massage. She says that till today. It makes me happy when I can give my loved ones relief or comfort from my hands.

I didn't like seeing the mermaid cry.

Tears of rain will find a seed that needs to grow
and when it grows, it will become a forest

I wanted to help the mermaid so much.

I knew she was very sad and I begged her to let me do the dishes. At first, she refused because she felt bad about letting me do it. But when she saw that I wasn't going to stop annoying her, she gave me permission to wash only the small ones. I had to leave the big ones because I couldn't hold them yet.

I felt so useful as I opened the blue tap at the back of the house and began to wash the vessels, feeling happy knowing I was making her job easier.

Hands can do so much if we let them serve

We couldn't believe it; we were going to see the dragon.

The separation had seemed so long in our minds and we asked the mermaid many unnecessary questions every day without fail.

"Will he recognize us?"
"Are we going to live there now?"
"Will we be going to a new school?"

She answered us patiently.

The mermaid started laughing once again. She was very pretty when she laughed.

It was exciting meeting the dragon in a new place. He got us lipstick candy, which made our day. We stayed with extended family friends who had kids—who were our age—so it was quite a lot of fun.

The dragon then took us on a tour and he pointed to the slopes of Darjeeling in the distance. How we stared… The clouds seemed to embrace the Himalayan range.

"Does God live there? And could we visit?" I asked the dragon.

Then I saw the snow…

How I longed to touch it, but it was impossible with our planned itinerary and would cost extra so I said a quick prayer…

"Please Lord, I hope it's not too much to ask but I'd love to see and touch snow someday. Amen."

**The Weaver hears everything and gives us what we ask
when we can appreciate it best**

I have not met a woman quite like the mermaid's friend.

She was an astounding, formidable woman of great substance. If anyone were to ask me why I believed in the Weaver, it is because of people like her who taught me that love and compassion can exist in a topsy-turvy world. The irony was that she didn't believe in Him, but I think in her heart she did, or rather had big fights with Him.

She was a victim of revenge. Acid was thrown on her as a little girl, leaving one side of her completely burned. She had just one eye, but through that she saw and appreciated the Weaver's creation in a way that I have not seen anyone else do. She enjoyed traveling, hiking, nature photography, and she was kind to the broken.

She often came to help the mermaid and made us promise to help out instead of squabbling amongst ourselves. We adored her and thought she was super cool; more so when she forbade us from calling her anything but Nutty Poopoo. She would sometimes rescue birds with broken wings (humans, actual birds or little animals) and it is by her example, that I understood how to value life, nature and the wild.

To me, she is the type of woman the Weaver allows to grace the Earth once in a lifetime to display His kind of love; the passionate kind that fights for the rights of the defenseless.

Those who are burned in fire become fire itself;
reborn from flames to light others' candles forever

Reena Doss

It had been a month since we returned home to Calcutta without the dragon, so it was exciting to know that his sibling's family was coming to visit us.

We did not expect the dragon would arrive before them. He was back with us for good. I don't think we could have been any happier.

We were together and our world was complete again.

A floating box travels to those who do not try to possess it

It had not happened before. My godmother and her family were coming to visit us from Bangalore.

I was thrilled to meet my three younger cousins. I loved hearing that the older boy was an exact replica of the dragon—when he was little—with his chubbiness and mad curly locks.

My older cousin from the mermaid's side had definitely influenced my sudden interest in organizing the unicorn, dolphin and little cousins to perform in homemade productions to entertain the grown-ups with fashion shows, concerts, comedy performances, skits, and singing.

I had a lot of fun exploring my interest in fashion growing up.

Everyone assumed that I would become a fashion designer.

The past shapes our roles for the future,
but it can't help us if we don't uncover its blessings

The unicorn, dolphin, and I had a modest collection of Barbie dolls.

Few were lovingly handed down to us, while the rest were thoughtful gifts. Since we didn't have a Ken doll, I remember creatively repurposing one of the older dolls by giving her a haircut, transforming her into our very own Ken. I even made dresses for the rest of them. I liked to do that periodically whenever I got bored with the old clothes. I would take old material, a needle and thread that the mermaid gave me and design and stitch my fashion collection to make it more interesting for storytelling.

With our doll family complete, I began weaving fairytales, using the dolls as characters. My first enthusiastic audience consisted of the unicorn and dolphin, who would listen with wide eyes and bated breath for what would happen next. As my storytelling skills grew, my godmother's children became ardent fans, requesting their favorite tales, which thrilled me. I would change my voice for different characters and laugh with pleasure when I noticed them sit up and pay even more close attention. Two cousins from the dragon's side would also visit us in Bangalore, eagerly gathering around to hear my stories. I cherished these moments, delighted to share my imagination with my dear family and friends.

None of them would leave until the main hero and heroine would kiss, which was basically a female Ken with a very baggy T-shirt (the handsome and devastating prince) and very beautiful Barbie (a mermaid princess and fairy), locked in a passionate embrace while I made the "muah-muah-muah" sound effects. After that moment, everyone would collectively sigh with audible satisfaction.

Gems of your heart can be pulled at will from the memories you collected

Our first TV was a tiny box with a knob and adjustment nodes on the side. Whenever the connection was disrupted, the dragon would head to the terrace to adjust the antenna, while I'd smack the TV or tweak the nodes, and the unicorn and dolphin would relay whether the signal improved. Once we found the right adjustment and *Doordarshan (DD) News* appeared, everyone felt satisfied.

The dragon was obsessed with cricket, so we knew that when sports, the Olympics, or tennis were on, we couldn't watch anything else. He was a big fan of Kapil Dev, Sachin Tendulkar, and many others. Later, when the mermaid started working and we upgraded to a new TV, we appreciated the value of color, having previously only seen black and white channels. The remote control wars were epic, with disagreements over what to watch after homework or on weekends. The dolphin didn't mind at the time, content to watch whatever we chose.

The dragon and mermaid also loved to watch *Miss India, Miss World and Miss Universe* every season so the unicorn, dolphin and I would also end up watching them. I suppose that did contribute to my fashion ideas for the Barbies we would play with and later on, in my raw sketches. I recall with fond amusement my cousin brothers' obsession with *Baywatch* and how everyone couldn't take their eyes of the women when they ran in slow motion in their skimpy bikinis. I always wondered how it managed to stay in place, being so high on their hips.

I vividly remember movies like *The Ten Commandments, Quo-Vadis, Ben-Hur, Brothers' Destiny, My Fair Lady, Roman Holiday, Breakfast at Tiffany's, Cleopatra, National Velvet, Lassie Come Home, The Quick and the Dead, The Godfather, Bushwhacked, The Musketeers, The Parent Trap*, and those films featuring travelers exploring the world through stamps.

Disney films were a huge hit in my world. We watched them on old tapes since they weren't frequently aired on our channels. The mermaid's family had left us a VCR player and few films, and later, friends from church gave us some during the transition from tapes to CDs/DVDs. I was also enthusiastic about watching *Cartoon Network* and *Nickelodeon* shows with the unicorn and dolphin, as well as *MTV* and *VTV* for music. We had many favorites!

Personally, I was more interested in watching *Narnia, Star Trek,* and *Batman and Robin* TV series.

Although we enjoyed Hollywood films, our household was familiar with Bollywood stars like Sharmila Tagore, Rekha, Shah Rukh Khan, Kajol, Anil Kapoor, Rani Mukerji, Madhuri Dixit, the Kapoor sisters, Amitabh & Jaya Bachchan, and more, thanks to the dragon and mermaid's love for cinema. They also watched Tamil movies in their mother tongue. I wasn't taught the language so I had no grasp of it. I think it's because they themselves didn't know it very well though the dragon liked to buy language dictionaries and study it by himself. I rarely watched Bollywood, but I do have my favorites. Perhaps it was due to my mental block with learning languages in school and having to study with the dragon at home.

Khoon Bhari Maang stands out in my mind; I saw it at my Grandy's when the dragon and mermaid were at church. Other favorites include *Mr. India, Amar Akbar Anthony, Kuch Kuch Hota Hai, Baazigar, 1942: A Love Story,* and *Dil To Pagal Hai.* Many of these movies' songs bring me joy when I hear them.

There were some movies that made me laugh so hard at the romantic corniness but that didn't stop me from watching them. It's incredibly difficult to explain why I loved romance and was at the same time, cynical of its existence. The villains would all die with one shot but if the heroes ever got critically injured, they would somehow last for 15 minutes after saying everything they wanted to. Then there were movies where the hero or heroine would get hit on the head and forget who they were until they were hit again at the exact moment they had to save the day. This would bring out the mischief in me and I would howl with laughter while at the same time, talk to the characters while watching TV, like "Just whack him on the head with that club and he'd remember".

Anjali left a lasting impression; I will not forget the song with the gentle repetition of "Anjali, Anjali, Anjali, little apple of the eye, apple of the eye, apple of the eye". Although I haven't seen *Minnale,* I recently discovered the heroine's name is Reena but the reason why I mention this here is because of the song *Vaseegara* that I love the most. I learned the lyrics from a classmate. Later, I found a Hindi version, but the original Tamil version has a unique tonal beauty that can't be replaced.

I could go on but these are the ones that come rushing to mind

It was our favorite show at the time. The unicorn, dolphin and I couldn't wait for the next episode whenever we visited the mermaid's friend after mass.

We loved the wolves, the raccoon, the monkeys, and Kaa, but our favorites were Bagheera and old Baloo (who was a free spirit without a care in the world).

I think I liked the dragon singing *Bare Necessities* the best though.

The Jungle Book TV series will capture anyone's imagination

The games the dragon taught us were legendary.

They included *Snakes and Ladders, Ludo,* and various card games like *Bluff, Donkey, Ass, Rummy, Literature, 7 Up, Thief, Last Card,* and more. He even took the time to teach us *Chess,* which I loved and still play occasionally when the mood strikes.

At school, during break times, I would play games like *Cat's Cradle, Hopscotch, Noughts and Crosses* with my classmates, and one of them even showed me how to play the snake game on a digital device.

I still chuckle when I think back to the *Ever Ready* battery brand, because whenever one died and we told the dragon we needed a new one, he'd say, "But how ready are you?" And we'd say, "Ever ready!" Quite gleefully too, I might add. And he'd laugh and say, "But I thought you were Dosses!" We would be dying with laughter by the time the dragon went to the store to get the new battery for us.

The dragon's jokes were never-ending

The dragon loved to play tricks. He enjoyed teasing us, but what I remember most is *April Fool's Day.*

No matter how old this trick was, we always fell for it. He would wake us up in the morning and tell us to hurry up or he would finish all the chocolates in the fridge. We would get up and race there, only to find it empty with the dragon cracking up at our expressions. We would scowl and sulk, completely annoyed. But when we got back home from school, he would have candy waiting for us.

We would run up to him, throw our arms around his neck or waist or legs and thank him.

I think he loved this part of his trick most of all.

Long hugs are the best kind of hugs

When the Monsoon season came that year to Calcutta, it carried on for days until it began to flood the streets around where we stayed. We were blessed that it did not seep into our home.

The unicorn, dolphin and I thought it was awfully exciting and the dragon and the mermaid distracted us from the seriousness of it by teaching us how to make paper boats and create bubbles from soap water.

They created magic for us in little moments.

Never underestimate little moments of magic;
they are the shield you will one day hold up to defeat evil

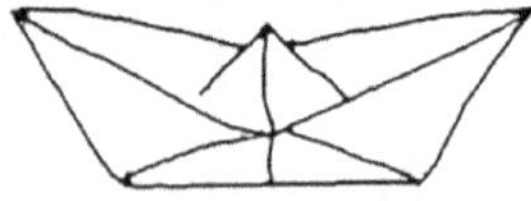

We found this amazing branded pastry shop called *Walls* right behind the street where we lived.

Whenever we could, the unicorn and I loved to go and stare at their window display. The smells were heavenly—full of cakes, assorted ice creams in mouthwatering colors, and who knows what else.

Once, the kindly old proprietor even offered us a free scoop of ice cream. I had to sadly decline and drag my reluctant unicorn away.

"No taking anything from strangers" had been drummed into our skulls. It was a tough choice to make, but neither one of us relished the trouble we'd be in with the mermaid and the dragon.

Hunger for a better life begins when you realize it is possible

Nana had a heart attack and was rushed to the hospital. But I just knew that she was going to get better. Nothing bad could happen to her heart. Her heart was good.

We slept at my uncle's home as all the adults kept coming and going. The dragon came back that day to get us ready. "Nana's gone", he said. I didn't understand what that meant, even when I saw Nana in a box with everyone lining up to kiss her hands or pay homage as the priest stood by.

I could hear the choir singing *Make Me a Channel of Your Peace.* I remember that song so vividly and felt so sad because I saw the mermaid crying.

Nana looked so peaceful, almost smiling, in that odd box. The dragon tilted me over and I kissed her cheek like I'd done so many times before. I felt her cold skin and that's when I knew. I remember bursting into tears. Everyone thought I was scared, but I wasn't. I just suddenly knew she wasn't there and that upset me more than anything else.

The dragon tried to comfort me, saying, "Sweetheart, she's in Heaven", but I didn't care.

I wanted her to read me *Heidi.* She'd promised she would the next time she came to stay. I wanted to listen to her tell me stories about the mermaid when she was my age. I wanted her to finish teaching me how to eat ripe mangoes without them dripping down her elbows (like how I ate them). I wanted to see her comb her hair and then shake out the loose strands and twist them into those neat little balls to be thrown away. I wanted her to confirm if squirrels took her teeth in the night or if she was a fairy dressed up as my Nana.

I hated Death. She was gone.

The only truth in our world is life and death
and what we do in between on that grand scale

At seven years old, I wanted to end my life.

I took the red-handled knife with the burned spot in the plastic and placed the tip on my belly. Alone in the long corridor, with no one home, I felt unseen and unheard. No one would care if I was not here, I thought. I would be forgotten. Everyone would get over it after the initial sadness.

I felt things so deeply—unwanted, unloved, and this strange internal pain that I wished would be physical instead. I thought it would be easy to get out of everyone's way. I don't remember what led to me even deciding to make this choice.

As I stood there, I saw something move from the corner of my eye, but as I looked, there was nothing. The desperation disappeared, and I dropped the knife, bursting into tears. I cried in a way I'm not sure other children my age could understand. There were no words for the pain I carried. I wanted to go to Heaven, and I was suddenly afraid I had ruined my chances. I fell to my knees, lifted my hands to the Weaver, and begged for forgiveness.

I could taste my breathing like as though I was a new self, separate from the other. For the first time, I felt like everything would be okay if I talked to Him about it. I wanted the gift of infinity with Him. Eternal life—that was my heritage. No one was going to take that from me, least of all—me. I promised Him I would not do that again and would always come to Him first.

I did not tell anyone about this because I felt ashamed and I feared I would be lectured without being heard. I had just killed the choice to steal my breath.

I had already begun scribbling in a diary. I would write, "I feel sad" or "I was angry" or I am happy". It read like a record of emotions experienced. I would name feelings but that day I discovered that I could also express the "whys" in ink.

I began my eighth year with a new sense of purpose

The dragon and the mermaid decided it was time to head back.

We were quite upset because we had made friends here, but we weren't going to complain. We trusted that they would not have made this choice if there had been a better one. We started again on that two-day train journey back to Bangalore.

Life was tough, but I was full of hope in things getting better.

I could find hope anywhere; even behind the paint peeling off the wall

During the transition period between pre-teen and teen years, I had a recurring dream about a tiger three times.

The first time it entered my home, I was paralyzed with terror at the way everyone was screaming, yet I wasn't afraid of it. The tiger's gold eyes turned and looked at me. It gleamed with the blue sky as it approached me, but I willed myself to wake up. I awoke with trembling hands.

The second time, I was engaged in a craft project when the tiger appeared. I did not see it at first until I saw its giant paws pacing around me. I slowly stood up, aware that the unicorn and dolphin were somewhere nearby. I asked the tiger how it dared to come inside without permission, but it only growled, sending chills down my spine. I noticed some of my papers lying in front of me and I waved them, trying to scare it away but I only succeeded in confusing it.

It pulled at the soft green curtains (that I had not seen in my life) before it darted out the window. It was then that I realized I wasn't in the city, and the forest stretched hazily out before me. I gazed into the dark woods to see if I could find the tiger. I felt an alarming urge to chase after it but pulled back, wondering what was wrong with me. Who in their right mind would chase after a wild animal?

The third time the tiger visited, I was in an unfamiliar bedroom. A part of me knew it was only a dream, so I felt I would be more prepared to face it. I asked the tiger what it wanted quite calmly but when it roared, my plan disappeared, and I felt afraid, sensing something deeper was happening. I tried to call my family, but they weren't there. The tiger seemed to have all the time in the world, and I was hypnotized by its presence. I looked into its eyes, now resembling the night sky, and knew I had to face the uncertain reality of death or discover if this was a dream I would wake from.

As I accepted my fate, the tiger roared in triumph, though it did not approach. It seemed to be waiting for something. Puzzled, I moved towards it and that was when it pounced. I woke up with a racing heart.

Years later, I searched for the dream's meaning but found nothing. Some dreams may not have meaning, while others don't leave your memory. You just know in your heart that you have to be patient because only time can reveal their significance.

The tiger had orange flames, blue-gray sky eyes, and white fur on its chest

I'd been maintaining my diary regularly.

I wasn't quite sure what to do with it, so I would end up documenting every inconsequential detail of my life and then would get mad when the unicorn and dolphin would read it and giggle like they knew all my secrets.

Didn't they read the painstakingly written words in red capitals saying "PRIVATE" on the front cover?

I hadn't met one cousin from the mermaid's side because he lived in France but when I found his baby picture, I sketched his portrait and kept it safely in my trunk to gift to him on the day when I would meet him. When the floods came, they destroyed it and a lot of my precious diaries as well. And I remember weeping for it felt like some part of me had died.

That didn't stop me from continuing to write.

One day, I realized my voice could be heard in the hallowed pages of my diaries.

One day, my words stopped being inconsequential things written down.

One day, I started writing about things that mattered, but not yet.

Some words were the clothes I wore on days
I couldn't speak joyfully about the world

I had just started learning the Hindi alphabet in Calcutta when we moved back to Bangalore.

To my utter dismay, the principal had assigned Hindi to me as my second language. The other choice was Kannada and I knew that would not help me because I had lost touch with the subject two years ago.

This put me at a massive disadvantage.

I was very discouraged as I struggled to blend in, unable to accept that I had now become a failure in the school where I once was a top-ranking student.

Failure at an early age instills compassion, patience, and the will to succeed

When we came back to Bangalore, we stayed with my godmother and her family for a month or so before we moved to a rented space.

We liked the new place a lot, especially since we now had beds and didn't have to sleep on mattresses on the floor anymore. That was a luxury and it felt like the Weaver was lifting us up a bit.

I became a performing monkey at future family get-togethers, but I enjoyed it. I grew used to being in charge of my little cousins from the dragon's side.

I thought my older cousin brothers were very cool as they rode bikes and did stunts on them. We were always delighted when they did take us for joy rides. This did not happen, however, when there were girls around whom they wanted to impress.

I managed to get a seat back in my old school, but I was not the same girl who had studied there before.

I shivered, feeling Autumn's chills, still processing the life-changing events of my summer days in Calcutta.

**When sadness seeps into the core of you,
there are things you begin to see that no one else can**

Before *Twinkle* died, she had two litters.

We took a black pup from the first litter and named her *Trixie*. She was a sweetheart, but we only had her for 8 months when the mermaid and the dragon said she had to go because she was causing too much damage at our rented home. The unicorn, dolphin and I cried, but there was nothing we could do.

Trixie II was from *Twinkle's* second litter, but the dragon and mermaid returned her the very next day when they found out that she was infested with fleas.

Trixie III we got from a friend down the street. She was a mix of a black Labrador and a roadation (I do not like calling them strays or street dogs) and had a half-white cross on her chest. We loved her dearly, but she died three years later. Someone poisoned her.

This was the final straw.

I didn't know how to handle the pain.

Trauma culminates to a crescendo in the unlikeliest of memories

Split

The harsh pang of losing someone I loved on this Earth
knowing I was not going to see them again
filled me with great pain

How unfamiliar it all was… How fragile were our lives…
How could we ever know what would happen in the future?

I considered the thought of losing
the dragon
the mermaid
the unicorn
and dolphin
and I felt frightened

I did not want to leave my shell
I would stay for as long as I could
for I was no longer desperate about leaving it

I wasn't too sure about the possibility of Heaven
I felt uncertain about
P R O M I S E S

Scars had appeared on my skin
the wind blew wild, dust settled in
weathering the time I had spent as
a Pearl
under a bleeding heart

cocoon

gathering new layers

III

CRACKED

Pearls in a nest don't crack until the winds of change arrive;
then twigs and bark dissemble as precious things get lost.

Torn

Learning   that
there's a whole other world   from the one I'd known
where people can be kind   if you let them in
even if Life teaches you   hard lessons
was something   new to me
I barely heard the crack   so soft its sound
when my safe world   was torn apart
and the infinite *sadness*   in the motions of time

house

swallowed me whole

We shifted again.

The new place had a chimney which was the height of all our childish dreams. The mermaid and the dragon would have preferred another place because the locality wasn't the best, but we had to make do with what we were given.

Besides, I don't believe there exists a child who didn't dream of Santa coming down the chimney.

Perhaps this time we'd find out how he did it.

**Struggles are a given, but their path is made easier
when you have an imagination that curls inside humor**

My first perfume was a gift from the dragon's oldest sister on my 13th birthday.

She would give us cards every year, and sentimental me would treasure them. I remember a letter that stood out. It was written on artsy paper and it said,

"Reena, pearls are for July-born girls,
and you are a pearl."

I was thrilled to receive the perfume bottle along with it. It was shaped like a beautiful woman, and was called *Lady Diana.* I made it last as long as possible. Wearing perfume made me feel grown up. It is a sensation that's hard to explain. Perhaps it's the subtle confidence boost, the feeling of elegance, or the sense of maturity that comes with it.

Whatever the reason, that first perfume marked a memorable milestone in my journey towards adulthood.

Why does wearing perfume make a girl feel like she's already a woman?

I shed my first blood. The mermaid had already prepared me when I questioned her about why the other girls had matured and I hadn't yet.

To be honest, I was relieved. I didn't want one more thing adding on to make me feel abnormal.

It was painful, the stomach cramps and severe migraines that followed.

And don't let me get started on the lectures… No hanging out with boys (that was not a problem), stay away from strange men, no need to kiss uncles on their cheeks when we greet them anymore (thank goodness!) and no sitting on any adult's lap, etc.

The list continued, but you get the picture.

Did boys undergo something similar too?

A girl's transition to womanhood comes with a lot of responsibilities

"Your house is too small for me to stay", she said one day, stunning me. I went home and cried because she had stayed with us so many times. What had changed?

The mermaid and the dragon consoled me, but I was deeply hurt.

"Please God", I prayed that night with the mermaid and the dragon beside us like always. "Please give us what we need daily. Protect us from evil and from those whose intentions and actions are not good. Bless our home and the people who help us directly or indirectly. Please take care of our family and send our guardian angels to watch over us, especially when we fall asleep each night. Please let me see the world and all you've made. Thank you for my family. Please give us a color TV, lots of toys, and a big house with our own rooms if that's okay with you. Amen."

I was full of faith.

The Weaver provides everything in good time

I started wearing my first bra.

I don't know why that made me feel like I was a woman, but it did. I didn't know that they would hurt during their growing stage if someone accidentally slammed into you or hit your chest. Since I wore those thin cotton bras, the shape of my breasts were still visible, and when outside, the mermaid would look at me in a very speaking way. I would find myself dragging my long hair in the front or hunching. I started to get more conscious of them as they grew because I noticed how men would look at me now, and I wished I could be flat chested again.

When I wore certain dresses, the mermaid would say, "Your chest looks too big in that," or any dress that went one inch above my knees, "That dress is too short to wear out". Soon, even the unicorn started repeating this when I would ask her how I looked after I got ready. I was always covering up, and I did not feel any freedom to dress in the way I wanted until I started working, which was years later, but even then, I would dress a whole lot more conservatively than the others. I kept wanting to hide myself without understanding where it was coming from.

The strange thing is that these same strictures didn't seem to apply to the unicorn and dolphin when they reached my age. I even had to wait to be allowed to do certain things, like watching certain movies or reading particular books, but when I earned that right via age, suddenly it was okay for the unicorn and dolphin to do the same. When I asked the mermaid why, she said, "It's because you are all different." I didn't think much of this explanation as it made no sense to me.

Even if outsiders told me I was beautiful, I wouldn't see it as a compliment. I saw only what the mermaid saw. A part of me felt a cooling from her as well, like as if she had erected some sort of wall between us after the traumatic incidents I had gone through. A part of me felt that if I didn't have breasts, maybe I wouldn't have been touched by my cousin, and the entire family's relationship with that side of her family would be intact. A part of me felt that if I didn't look pretty, the stranger at the exhibition wouldn't have molested me. If only… If only… If only…

Not once did I think, until I was an adult, that none of those incidents were my fault, that I shouldn't have had to navigate such painfully upsetting situations by myself, or even go through further trauma when I started speaking up about it.

There I was—12-year-old me, 13-year-old me, 14-year-old me, 15-year-old me, mocked for looking like I carried the world on my shoulders and at the same time trying to please those I loved. I broke this pattern later on in life though by taking the first step—sticking up for myself, even if I had to do it alone.

The self-criticism, shame and judgement fractured my mind
of ready ink into a million shapes of beauty

I tried to scream, but I couldn't.

The man was a stranger, yet I felt the intimate violation of myself as I stood behind the mermaid at that crowded public fest. He mocked my helplessness as his large, cruel hands pinched my budding peaks. That hurt. Badly.

I screamed. The man smirked again as he made his way behind me and manhandled my derriere.

I screamed again, but my screams were silent as tears trickled down my face. He grabbed my left breast and squeezed it. I didn't understand why he did that.

I screamed louder this time. Why couldn't anyone hear me?

The dragon, the unicorn and dolphin were at another stall.

"Mama!" I called, not realizing my voice was soft. I tried again.

"Mama!" I said, more loudly. "Mama!"

"Mama!" I called again, my voice now elevated in fear, as the man continued his assault.

She was watching the demonstration of some housing equipment along with the crowd.

Terrified, unable to speak, embarrassed because everyone was looking at me in disgust like I was a badly behaved brat, I shook my head like it was nothing.

The man deliberately slid his hand between my legs and rubbed me roughly. I tried to push him, but it was ineffective. I was not strong enough to fight him. I stood silently, tears flowing as he continued to abuse my body.

When the crowds began to thin, the man disappeared. I can't remember his face, but I will not forget his eyes. He left me screaming in a rage so potent, it buried me under rubble.

I felt let down by the mermaid, by the dragon, and by the Weaver.

No one saved me. I was very angry.

It was also the first time I had dressed up and felt pretty.

**The art of invisibility is achieved by practice;
camouflage your body and appear boring**

One summer stands out distinctly.

The mermaid's brother and wife offered us their old black Fiat, so the dragon, a driver, and two of my cousins embarked on a trip to collect it. Meanwhile, since the mermaid was working at her new job during the day, the dragon's sister and husband took us to their home in Kerala for the holidays.

We had an amazing time, as it was just the unicorn, dolphin, my cousin, her little sister, and me. My cousin braided my hair into several thin plaits so I could get curls when I removed them which was fun. My aunt even got us involved with art projects where we made collages from magazines and she took our pictures as well to make sure we remembered these times. We enjoyed painting, playing games, chatting late into the night, watching movies, celebrating the dolphin's birthday, savoring paper dosas as large as a table, dining at fancy restaurants, and visiting the beach.

During one of these outings, I rescued my little cousin from venturing too far into the water. Notably, I didn't know how to swim myself, but I went in after her and grabbed her before the water closed in over her tiny self—a moment she still remembers to this day. As we sat in the train compartment to go back home, my youngest cousin started howling which made us also cry. We did have a great time.

Inherent softness is like a marker of peace;
it strums a harmony to remind you to pass it on

He was trusted and adored when he visited our home one night, and while the dragon and mermaid slept, came to us as we lay fast asleep. I thought it was the mermaid pulling the blanket to cover me when I woke from my slumber to notice that a hand had pulled back the cover and was moving with deliberation over my barely developed chest.

But that was not the worst of it. It was when I twisted around to see who it was.

Him…

I didn't dare look below his waistline, but I thought I saw something I shouldn't have, as he stood crouched behind the door, terrified of being recognized.

I was too scared to scream. The unicorn and dolphin were near me. I turned on my front and lay very still, waiting. He darted across the hall from where we slept toward the restroom and I raced to the bedroom, shaking and telling the dragon and mermaid what he had done.

The mermaid and the dragon were shocked, but he denied it and had the guts to say I probably dreamed the whole thing up. I didn't understand why I couldn't look him in the eye and yell. Why was I protecting him? I was so confused. I was a child still. He was ashamed so he left immediately, but acted like he was the insulted party instead.

I wanted to curl up inside and die.

Why did you choose me? I adored you.

Betrayal by someone you trust is worse than the act of being molested

No matter how bad the other molestations were, he had hurt me the most because he was someone I had trusted.

The mermaid told me to forgive them all. How I tried, every single day… But all that came from my heart was a prayer that he should catch a break at work and go far, far away.

The Sun heard my prayer because it happened.

I couldn't believe it when he came to visit us a few years after the incident. How we sat to dinner with the entire family as if nothing had happened. It seemed like I was the sulky, moody girl when I was a survivor.

He bought us earrings. *How did that change anything you did?*
Ugh, I hated them.

I was so mad and I prayed so hard for his success because I knew the Sun alone understood how much I both loved and hated my molester. I struggled with my inability to forgive him when the nightmares would come. I hoped to forgive him, but I was unable to until I looked at him through the eyes of an adult in my later years.

Forgiveness found its own way, freely offered this time to eyes that begged for it. I wondered if perhaps I had saved him from his path that night by speaking up.

The greatest weapon against evil is forgiveness
because it heals bitterness and unblocks untold blessings

They mocked me for being jumpy and scared of being touched, called me "a delicate darling" and tried to make me feel bad about my newly acquired sensitivity to touch. I think it's because they didn't believe me when the mermaid told them about how he touched me that night as I slept with the unicorn and dolphin.

"Oh, she must have read some romantic novel and imagined this up!" they said like as if my daydream of a handsome knight involved my older cousin brother, creeping towards the bed that I shared with the dolphin to touch my barely there breasts. They didn't know this ugly side to him and believed, instead, that I was the liar because most people saw me as the child who daydreamed. They themselves had had negative experiences, so how could they have not had the compassion to see that I was the one who had been betrayed; not just by him, but by them too. Somehow, that made it so much more worse.

Over the years I learned to block this but when I started speaking up about it, I was amazed to be told to keep quiet, to not make it someone else's burden and then the final straw, "It happened to you, not us."

Have you ever experienced the sorrow of knowing that the betrayal of one connects so many more in the dark?

More people I loved sided against me.

Making a child disbelieve the reality of what they experienced just because adults cannot face the truth is a crime

I had a recurring dream. I kept falling and I would wake up before I hit the ground. This dream increased in its frequency and I found it hard to sleep.

Often, I would get up at the slightest sound. When I did sleep properly, I would wake up sweating from a nightmare or the falling dream.

Sometimes, I thought I saw an incredible bright light so I would pretend that I had been dreaming of Nana and the angels.

Stress and anxiety built up inside and became a part of my world

I adored my older cousin sister.

She would spoil us rotten, kiss and hug us regularly like we were her special babies.

Her heart was as big as an ocean and I always felt loved by her. She would comb my hair, braid it, scold and encourage me.

She would come to see us in Bangalore whenever she could and I would look forward to those visits because she had the most adventurous stories and took an interest in each of us.

As I grew, I think she forgot that we weren't children anymore and did not need her protection though I appreciated and remembered everything she did for us. Her kindness was something I kept close in my heart.

She changed her affection towards us after incidents happened and it saddened me but I understood that this was life.

Memories can sometimes take the shape of a fluid river
that will inevitably run into a waterfall

Sometimes the stars would overwhelm me and shape my dying world with their exquisite finery.

How did they twinkle like fine diamonds when there was so much blackness surrounding them?

The way the winds blew gently on the terrace; caressing my face, drying my tears, inviting me to look beyond what I was seeing in that kind, listening silence.

As I looked, I saw the dancing palm trees, heard the crickets chirping, felt the breeze tenderly play with my hair, smelled the fresh earth after the first Monsoon rain and I found myself thanking the stars.

I knew in that moment that I too was designed by the same Creator for a purpose unknown yet. I was part of something big and I knew with great certainty that the Weaver existed.

**The stars share their greatest secret
when they illuminate the presence of the Weaver**

There was a grotto of *Our Lady* in school.

I loved going there to talk to Mother Mary. I always felt peaceful gazing at her.

I would look away and quickly look back at her, certain that she would blink or move and I could catch her. I sometimes felt a soft chuckle next to me and I was immediately certain she was present, laughing, and playing this game with me. This did not make me frightened at all because I felt so protected and loved in those moments.

I knew then that she was not in the statue, but I still liked to visit it.

The Queen Of Sorrows comforted me

I was afraid of the thought of being touched by a man because I could not separate the pain I had experienced at the hands of my abusers with that of the promised One.

I made a solemn promise to the Weaver that I would save myself for my future husband, despite the fears I struggled with and the pressures of the world that I knew would come my way.

I left my anxieties with a childlike trust in His capable hands.

A vow made to the Weaver is a sacred promise

I first saw *Titanic* almost two years after its release.

The theaters were still playing it everywhere, and I would keep asking the dragon to see it whenever we passed the billboard near the bus stop close to the old theatre near Brigade's. The unicorn would back me up on this request, as we had become curious from overhearing our classmates talk about the movie.

Everyone was in love with the hero and wanted to marry him, which I found rather absurd because I saw no logic in that, even though my romantic side softened with understanding. The yearning to be so deeply loved was a universal need, but when they started talking about the film, I would block my ears because I wanted to experience it without knowing how it would end. The tickets were expensive, and I knew it wouldn't be possible, but I would still ask.

That's why I was surprised when the dragon agreed on that particular day. The prices had come down. It was pure luck or was it fate's coincidence? I was thrilled because it would be my first theatre experience. Plus, we would all be going as a family, which was another wonderful first. Though I forgot the name of the theater, I do remember it was the one close to Brigade's that eventually got shut down. It was and will always be one of my favorite movies of all time.

I was blown away by the love story, the emotions that swept me away, and the bittersweet ending that shows love cannot die when it is experienced, given, and received mutually. Whenever the kissing or nude scenes were on, the dragon and mermaid got anxious and asked us to close our eyes immediately. We tried to obey them, doing our best to cover our eyes while giggling, but sometimes, we peeked.

All of us were deeply affected by the film in different ways. On the bus ride home, I was quiet, my eyes welling up with tears. "It's not real," the dragon and mermaid teased, amused. The unicorn nudged me, "Hey, it's just a movie," she said, then whispered, "But even I feel sad." The dragon marveled at the cinematic effects and realism. The mermaid reminisced about the passengers' back stories, like the elderly couple embracing in bed, waiting for the waters to take them. Then I heard them discussing why Jack and Rose couldn't fit on the floating door. That scene made sense to me though even if I hated that it had to happen. Of course, he couldn't get on. He tried before he decided to make that sacrifice and Rose had to let him go when the time came to honor that sacrifice.

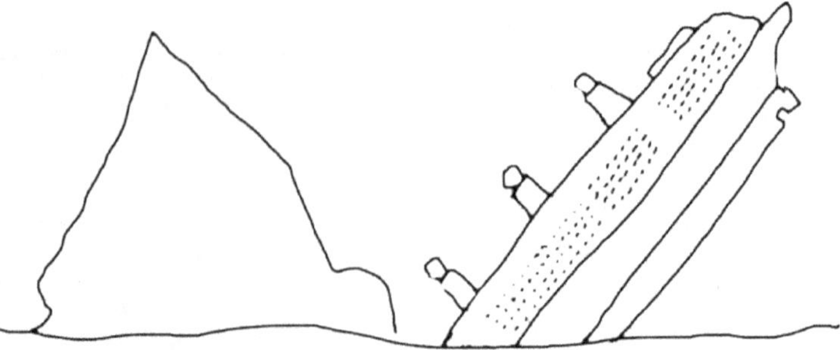

The dolphin, deep in thought, asked the unicorn and me why Jack and Rose were naked and why their kisses looked like they were trying to eat each other. We laughed awkwardly, unsure how to answer. We repeated her question to the dragon and mermaid, hoping for insight. The dragon said it only happens in movies, and the mermaid said we'd understand when we got older. We teased the dolphin, but I had many questions. Did the dragon and mermaid kiss like that? Why were they without clothes? What were they doing in the car?

That night, when everyone was asleep, I found myself crying and whispering a small prayer. I thanked the Weaver for letting us see the movie, and despite knowing it was just a film, I asked Him to make sure Jack didn't drown in the ocean but somehow survived and had a happily ever after. I also prayed for my person, wherever he might be. This was the first time I remembered including my future husband in my prayers.

Later in life, I learned that when we surrender to the Weaver's plan and live our lives with openness, He weaves magic into our journey, paying close attention to the details.

The Weaver is a gatherer of all prayers, wounds and fears

I was completely enchanted with the song *My Heart Will Go On* by Celine Dion.

But now come to think about it, it was the stunning instrumental music and vocalizing that seemed to reach into the depths of me and give me space to feel something I just couldn't place at that age.

Every time we had a family gathering or a party, the dragon would ask me to sing this. I didn't have access to the internet, so I had to learn the song the old-fashioned way— by listening to it repeatedly and trying to decipher the lyrics. For a long time, I sang the song with incorrect lyrics, much to the amusement of my family, I'm sure. It wasn't until the mermaid's good friend's daughter wrote down the correct lyrics for me that I was finally able to sing it correctly. I still have that piece of paper because I knew she didn't have to but she did.

I memorized the words by heart and would often sing it to the unicorn and dolphin after we said our prayers "to help them sleep" or so they claimed. But in reality, I think they just loved to throw their hands and legs on me so I would tickle them as I sang.

The music of love opens doors you cannot even imagine

There was a biweekly Church meeting at the Cathedral and I asked the dragon if I could go with him too. He agreed.

This place literally saved me by teaching me how to see my past—and the bad things that would happen in the future—through eyes of faith, rather than from a heart that could have frozen in fear.

The catechizes helped me hold fast to my values during difficult times and gave me the foundation I required to apply the reality of my faith. When I realized I had to re-evaluate my understanding of the Weaver, I was greatly surprised.

He was not the Weaver whom I thought I had known. He was more, so much more.

I fell in love with the Weaver Of The Celestial Sky

In a little boat, who would you rely on to calm the seas of others?

When I was 11, I joined the Neo-Catechumenal catechisms at church with the dragon, who was initially doing it in secret until the mermaid found out. She then allowed me to attend, as I immediately begged to join him. After a few weeks, the mermaid started accompanying us, seeing how happy we were. Usually, the age to join was 13 and over so when the community group formed, I was permitted to join even though I had just completed my 12th birthday. This was likely due as well to my perceived maturity but as an old soul, I wasn't surprised.

Initially, everything was wonderful. I made friends easily, and we all had a great rapport. However, as I hung out more with them, I began to experience the demons of jealousy, resentment and cruelty from others touch me. I felt isolated again, unable to understand why. When I tried to address these issues, I was told to change and conform to their behavior which included gossip and mocking others. I refused. I knew that it wasn't me. And thus, I became the punching bag, an easy target or so they thought. But bullies often underestimate the quiet ones. The longer I stayed, I felt drained. It took me years to leave the community and it wasn't because of the good that was being catechized, it was just that there was a lot of toxicity and things I noticed that I knew was not right. It wasn't easy to leave—but when I did, the judgment, criticism and condemnation I faced made it more clear to me that there was a lot more ego running things, than allowing Christ to lead. That's when I understood that the Weaver had a different plan for me but without those encounters, I wouldn't have learned about the darkness that lurked in human nature. The valuable teachings I took away from these years gave me a strong foundation for my next life chapter.

I also learned more lessons about love and realized I wanted someone brave, someone who would be proud to be with me and unwilling to settle for less. These experiences taught me that people's actions that don't correspond with their faith cannot have a say in my personal connection and relationship with the Weaver. It didn't matter what anyone said.

In my heart, I knew that Jesus loved me as I am, where I was going and what I was going to be. I was not letting go of His hand but I certainly was letting go of everyone who told me that He wouldn't be there for me if I left.

Instilling fear through insults, manipulative tactics and controlling lives was not going to keep me chained to those whose pride in their importance was more significant. They seemed to have forgotten what they had started the community for and I was ready to explore my faith in a more profound way.

I clung tightly to the Weaver as I stepped bravely into the world and came face to face with demons, battles and temptations. I would not have survived them if I hadn't kept my integrity nor would my gifts have received their exercise in order to be of service to the one who gave them to me. Anyone can pray, attend church, and appear holy but still be monsters in disguise, holding a false light. Only after facing your own demons can you stand firm in life's storms.

In a small boat, He sits with me and calms the seas of my heart

My first crush ignored me, breaking my tender heart.

I learned for the first time how the world was and that inevitable change—though painful—was necessary.

The laughable truth was that my heart had no clear idea of what it wanted yet… when I moved on to my second crush.

The heart is a fickle thing until it knows how to love selflessly

The boy was considered arrogant, but I knew he was just shy.

Once when we were all playing together, she dressed me up as a bride for a wedding she had planned with him as the bridegroom. It was a game, but I'm not sure what she meant by that.

I remember feeling upset and confused so I ran away. Brother and sister did not talk properly to me after that. Even as adults.

I understand why now.

Some unexplained events get explained with time

I was a good child growing up, but I was a horrendous teenager.

I had stored a lot of anger inside me and it came out during these years when I would yell back at the dragon and mermaid. It was the dragon who approached me with uncommon understanding and love, and though I knew that what he said was often right, I fought all the more with him, pushing his limits. The dragon somehow managed to show great restraint and patience; recognizing my anger came from deep-rooted pain.

But when the dragon and I were at loggerheads, it was the mermaid who would remind me of what a gem of a man he was and it did not fail to calm my raging waters.

I was a half-moon who discovered I held an ocean,
but did not yet know how to control its tides

I suppose he was a water soul, for that's where he eventually found rest later in life, but not during this period.

Summer holidays brought the dragon's brother's kids home, and we got into all sorts of mischief, playing games and laughing until our stomachs ached. I think we were all thrilled to have them, as we longed for brothers. They were curious, asking questions that made me ponder answers.

The oldest was a deep thinker and being around the dolphin's age, naturally paired up with her for playtime. The middle one was my favorite, as I sensed a kindred old soul spirit in him. He was poetic, witty, and sharp, but had a soft side that I knew the world might not be kind to, so I prayed he'd find the courage to preserve it. The youngest had a temper, but outgrew it later on. He'd follow the unicorn, who couldn't resist his charms, but his singing would awaken something deep within me. His voice was clear, vibrant, and rich with emotion. As a kid, he loved singing *Ayesha,* and I'd always request it.

I mention the youngest for special reasons because I saw him grow into a fine young man who viewed the world through beautiful lens and who died heroically, trying to save lives. He was the sweetest, most thoughtful, and kind soul you'd ever meet, with a quietness that encouraged peace. You'd know it by the way he made you feel.

Missing until we meet again

The mermaid once lost her temper with me for calling my unicorn the dreaded "B" word but what made her angrier was the fact that I lied about it and did not even know what it meant. I was not happy with the unicorn for tattling on me. I got the belt as punishment.

The dragon once shook me so badly that I could hear my teeth rattle. I had run after my dog—who had taken off when the gate was open—and had ended up in a questionable locality. I was so happy when I found her that I could not understand why the dragon's hands were trembling or why he was so angry with me. I was upset with him for a long time—even though he apologized—until the mermaid explained that he had been terrified of losing me that day.

If we argued back or did any mischief, it meant kneeling down until we said sorry—which I would stubbornly refuse to do, even though my unicorn would beg me to so we could play. I did not like it when the dragon or the mermaid would get angry with me.

The dragon was very strict when it came to completing our homework. He did not hesitate to use the wooden scale.

I used to be able to write with both hands, though I would favor the left, but the dragon insisted that I use my right hand while learning to write because it was the proper thing to do. He had been taught this too in childhood and so he made me practice writing every day. This was a rule I had to follow because the teachers had also complained about my handwriting. I do not know if I started self-sabotaging myself at some point just to prove something even though that did not lead anywhere.

I did not enjoy any of these experiences.

I hated it.

Left or right-handed or ambidextrous; how did it matter?

Chicken pox was the worst.

The unicorn and the dolphin thought they were immune until they got it too from purposely touching me when I warned them not to. But the dragon and the mermaid were glad that we got it as kids, instead of as adults. Neem baths, no school, TV, ointment to dry the boils, and getting yelled at about not scratching the scabs were part and parcel of this tiresome pox.

Catching up with school work was the bigger challenge because once you get chicken pox, you won't ever get it again.

The unicorn, dolphin, and the moon were a handful

The dragon and mermaid would bring home a variety of biscuits, including Parle-G, Britannia Marie Gold, Jim Jam, and Bourbon. Jim Jam and Bourbon were my absolute favorites! I fondly remember licking the cream first and then dipping the biscuits in my milk or Horlicks.

As kids, our allowed drinks were Cola, Thumbs Up, Limca, Fido Dido, 7UP, Milk, and Horlicks; tea and coffee were off-limits until I started having them in college. I loved the Fido Dido ads and thought they were super creative. I loved how they blended simple sketch animations into real life situations. Their ads were so relatable. The *Thumbs Up* ad also had a fun catchy phrase "Taste the thunder" with all the storm effects so when I first tried it, I expected thunder to boom in my ears and lightning to flash on my tongue. Instead, it built up in my belly. That had a comical effect on the unicorn, dolphin and dragon as we would all go into peals of laughter each time one of us let out "the thunder". The mermaid was too much a lady for that nonsense and off she would go to the kitchen.

On special days, the dragon would surprise us with Kwality ice cream from an ice cream cart or softee ice cream from Iyengar's Bakery or an egg puff from Thom's Bakery on Saturdays after church. When we were younger, he'd treat us to Mango Frooti, just like in the ad we loved. The mermaid would often fry finger chips or papadam to enjoy with our meals. We'd get excited when it was finger chips, wearing them like finger gloves to eat them slowly just for fun!

When we were in Calcutta, I recall how we'd indulge in delicious Kati rolls from dhabas—though they've become less generous in size and fillings over time.

I cherished saving paisas to buy sweets and treats from the school canteen or nearby shop, like Badam ice cream sticks, Ice Lollies, Big Babool, Poppins, Mango Bite toffees, Mentos, Tic Tacs, Chicklets, Cadbury Gems, or Diary Milk chocolates.

Remembering these delightful childhood moments still makes my mouth water!

We were cleaning the house when we saw it.

I had pulled the trunk away from the wall and the unicorn had climbed on top of it and was using the broom to sweep behind it all the way to the stacked boxes in the corner, which acted like our TV table. She suddenly turned to me and asked me to hold the broom as she held the edge of the box to pick up the brown belt she saw lying there. When she picked it up, the belt moved, causing her to drop it as we both realized that it was a snake. We both screamed for the dragon and mermaid.

Lassie was the first one to hear and she came charging towards the box, but I dropped the broom and grabbed her collar. The dolphin jumped down from the box and pulled me towards the door of our bedroom. The dragon was inside the other bedroom and the mermaid was outside, but they also came running to the hall.

The dolphin was trying to peek around us when the mermaid who had sized up the situation, quickly gave us instructions. She told us all to get inside our rooms, lock our doors, and put our laundry clothes in between the gap. Frightened but also excited, we did as we were told. The dragon did the same; he was quite scared but the mermaid was in lioness mode. She was brave.

After asking the neighbors if they knew of anyone they could call, she took the initiative of picking up the broom and trying to get it out. Apparently, it tried to get into our rooms but could not, thanks to the mermaid's quick thinking.

When the neighbor brought a snake catcher on his bike (which, by the way, I found so incredible that he was able to find one in a matter of an hour), there was a crowd gathered. The mermaid tells the events after this so well, so if you ever visit us, you must ask her to tell you the chucklesome aspects of this story; she was truly the heroine of it. After the poisonous snake was caught and bundled off to be released in the woods, we all heaved a heavy sigh of relief.

Once again, we saw another one in that same month. This time, the dolphin spotted it when she was sitting with the dragon. Luckily, we were all inside the house, and from the window, we could see it gliding on the wall next to the drumstick tree, but it moved over our wall and onto the street. When the mermaid questioned a neighbor about it, the lady told her it was a common occurrence; some were poisonous and others were quite harmless.

The mermaid was speechless at how casually the explanation was given. The unicorn, dolphin, and I collapsed with laughter because, to us, it was like we were living in the wild.

Do you know how many monkey families have visited us apart from snakes?

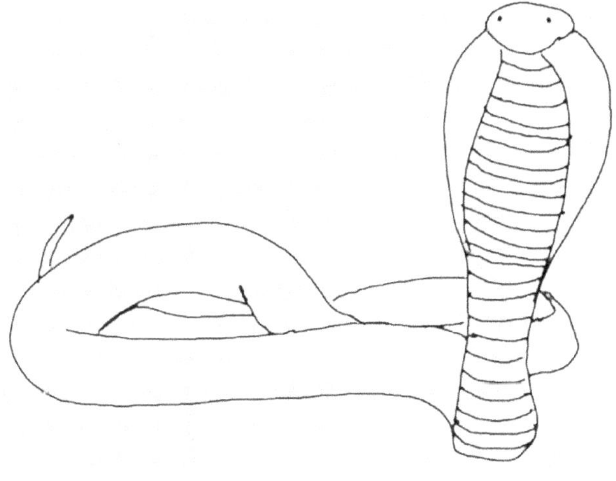

I was comparatively naïve given what I had experienced.

The dragon and mermaid were too embarrassed to tell us the facts of life, as it were. I heard snippets, but felt no real interest to know. It just felt gross and I already had a twisted notion brewing in my head about men. But if you had asked me to explain that, I would not have been able to.

When I learned the mechanics of sex, I was not impressed. I was quite annoyed that people made such a big deal about it.

Truth was that I was terrified, but I acted disgusted and disinterested. I felt it protected me from anything happening.

It was difficult for me to see this as something good.

Abuse had painted a black shield over my eyes

I cherished the Sunday Lauds tradition, where we prayed together as a family.

The dragon would randomly select a gospel reading, and we'd prepare the table with flowers and the holy books. We'd take turns reading prayers, psalms, and responsorial pieces, creating a sense of unity and solidarity.

However, this tradition gradually deteriorated into a performance, where imperfections were mocked, disagreements became about who was right and sharing vulnerably made you want to curl back into your shell. Egos were always pacified, and fears, tears, and anxieties only grew. I lost enthusiasm for this, but my desire to pray remained.

I wanted to learn the rosary, remembering the mermaid praying with us when we were young. I tried to pray it alone but found it boring due to my lack of understanding. I asked the mermaid to teach me again and to restart our family prayers, but it did not happen. Years later, I learned how to pray the rosary through online resources after getting reintroduced to it at my Aunt's.

In my conversations with Jesus, I always felt comforted, laughed with, and guided. I refused to abandon prayer or my faith due to past disillusionments. Instead, I asked Jesus to teach me how to pray, so I could one day share this joy with my future spouse and children, transmitting faith in a way that feels accepting because that is how the Weaver teaches.

When mature faith steps in, the pedestals of idolatry crumble

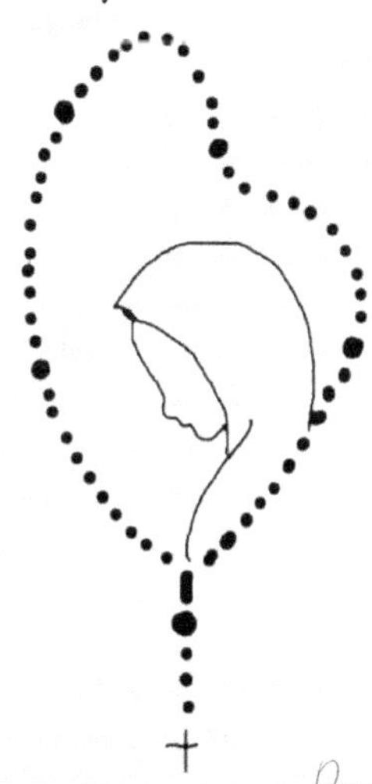

Traveling by autorickshaw still has a certain charm when in Bangalore city.

Since we didn't have a car, we traveled mostly by public transport, which was often the bus or the autorickshaw. For non-family events, the dragon would use his bike. The bus stories are a saga all on their own and they would occur in my college and university years.

The most absurd part about catching an auto was how much power they seemed to be tripping on. You would think that as a profession, it is their job to take you places where you need to go.

But no, over here, they will ask you where you want to go and if it isn't where they were going, they'd say no and carry on. Or they would ask for extra. Some of them will be empty and will see you waving your hand at them but they will look the other way and keep going.

If it starts raining, they won't move an inch. They will be sleeping inside on the passenger's seat with a rug, having a hot cup of tea and smoking a rolled up cigarette. You could be drenched and they will look their nose down at you and say in the most reasonable voice you ever heard,

"It's raining, ma'am."

And if you insist, they will say, "Okay, but you have to pay double over the meter fare". If you ask why again, they will say,

"It's raining, ma'am."

If you ask, "But why double?" They will reply very logically,

"It is raining, ma'am",

like as if this simple explanation covers every possible question you could think of.

At times, I would often find myself wanting to laugh at the ridiculousness of it or I would entertain myself with an image of Bangalore snowing and the auto drivers leveling up on their excuses.

Thank goodness for travels apps like Ola, Namma Yatri, and Rapido that are available today.

I call the autos the mini-dons of our streets

A doctor predicted that I might have a heart problem.

Everyone prayed nothing would happen to me. She was wrong in her diagnosis, but right about the abnormality of my heart rate. I wish she'd said something about the oddity of a girl my age carrying too much stress.

I kept feeling that there was something wrong with me.

I can't imagine how I would have coped
if I did not have words or art to save me

There was a boy next door who had a crush on me. The unicorn knew it and directly asked him if that was true. He confessed, much to my surprise and confusion.

We moved soon after and he cycled every week for two months to hang out because he missed us. The unicorn and dolphin teased me about it and said he only came because of me.

Nothing ever happened. I didn't like him that way and I didn't encourage further visits even though he asked.

You see, I wasn't sure I could trust men except for the dragon.

Maybe I would become a nun and live in an orphanage?

I didn't like most of the nuns I came across.

They were rude, stuck up and mean. How could they claim to love God when their behavior dictated otherwise? They seemed to be focused on acquiring money, funds for things that didn't seem necessary and embarrassing students over simple things. Occasionally, if they were in a good mood, we wouldn't be pulled up for acting out of line.

Special treatment was given to certain children and they were pushed to stand out in events they had no interest in. The ones who couldn't afford certain luxuries or give donations to the school were ignored. I noticed all these subtleties carefully to ponder about later. I saw the darkness in things I shouldn't have needed to. I saw the duplicity of duality in people that weren't aware of it themselves.

I remember two nuns. One from primary school and one in high school. I liked them both quite a lot because it certainly seemed to me that they didn't fit in with the others. We could approach them and it was easy to see how much they loved talking and teaching children.

Money taught tongues to sing. Money made bodies dance to the giver's tunes. Money bought fake smiles.

The thrill of upgrading to fountain pens was palpable!

I remember the excitement of filling my pen with ink from the bottle, watching as the liquid flowed into the nib, ready to bring my thoughts to life on paper. It was a rite of passage, a sign of growing up and leaving pencils behind.

But, as with any new skill, challenges arose. I soon discovered that mistakes were no longer easily erased with a simple pencil eraser. Without the convenience of a white correction fluid pen, I turned to a two-sided eraser, hoping to correct my errors. However, the eraser's abrasive side often proved too harsh, leaving holes in the page instead of erasing the mistakes. Panic set in as I frantically tried to repair the damage. In a desperate attempt to avoid my teacher's wrath, I would tear out the flawed page, only to realize that I had to remove its identical twin as well, to maintain the notebook's symmetry. The fear of my teacher's punishment, which included getting beaten on the legs with a scale, drove me to take such drastic measures.

Looking back, it seems almost funny, but at the time, it was a serious matter, and I was determined to avoid that at all costs!

Physical punishment was so common in school that we as kids suppressed how we felt about it

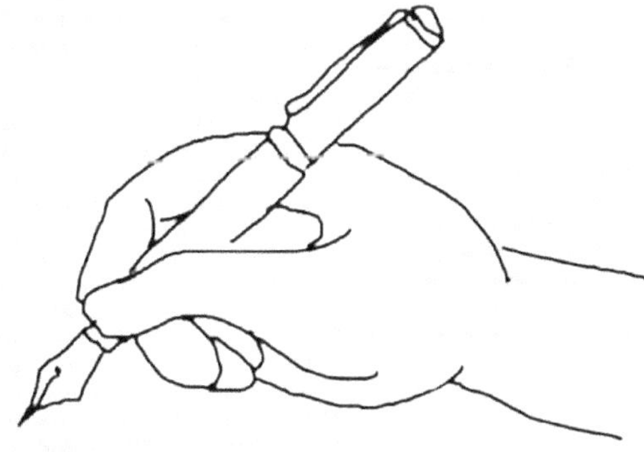

Every year, my classmates who celebrated *Diwali* would eagerly look forward to the fireworks and so did we.

The dragon would get our fireworks from a vendor who sold them near the army quarters, which became our go-to destination for three consecutive years. How we loved the fountain, the spinning wheel and sprinkler fireworks! The dragon would allow us to enjoy a few, and he'd save the rest for Christmas.

However, we had heard disturbing cases where some fireworks were being made by the small hands of impoverished or abandoned children. Moved by these concerns, the mermaid decided to put an end to our firework celebrations, and the dragon agreed. Initially, we didn't understand, but later on we realized that this was a good decision. The continuous use of fireworks by millions were causing massive issues like noise and air pollution as well as cases of poisoning.

The world has a collection of religions, many ways of learning the truth and practicing traditions. I am blessed to have many friends from various paths that have shown me more about my faith than I ever learned from those who were from the religion I was from.

It is how I learned through life—from brokenness, kindness, cruelty, generosity, selfishness, loved ones, enemies and strangers—that there is only one God who answers me in any crisis or joy that I experience. He isn't my religion, He is my light, my salvation, my hope and my peace. He is *Jesus Christ,* my best friend, my brother and the unconditional love that walks steadily with me, pointing the way, correcting me gently when I need it and pouring love into my soul, even if all others forget or do not.

When you let Weaver enter the place where evil took you away from Him, the connection to Him will be healed

When I first started hearing the "thees" and "thous" of *Shakespeare,* I was at once revolted because I just didn't get it.

The dragon loved the language and he changed my mind when he would recite *Mark Anthony's* speech by heart, much to my awe and delight. I think this was the only time I enjoyed studying with the dragon because his enthusiasm for the poetic verses inspired my love for poetry to the point where the hidden language of this great playwright started to make itself known to me. Before I knew it, I was a duly converted *Shakespearean* fan.

After reading all his works, I moved to the mermaid's hidden treasure in her trunk of books. I could give you a 30 page list but my favorites were the historical romance works of *Georgette Heyer,* which would eventually have a massive influence on my life.

That assorted collection of books in that old army trunk became my best friends through many a stormy weather.

I still enjoy living in the worlds that Georgette Heyer created

"Are you from Thailand?" I heard our Geography teacher's voice boom as it sliced through the busy silence, startling all of us.

We had been given the task of plotting a map and were so absorbed in that assignment that her presence so close to my desk made me jump and panic before I even understood the question. It seemed out of place with what we were doing, and I looked up at her, feeling quite puzzled. To my relief, she wasn't glaring at me with that "I'm going to squish you" expression on her face but at the girl in the parallel row.

The girl in question was completely ignoring the fact that the teacher and all of us were looking at her. "Well?" repeated the irate teacher.

The girl's neighbor elbowed her furiously. Casually, the girl glanced at the teacher, and then said sarcastically, "Well, what?" This seemed to aggravate the teacher some more.

"Are you from Thailand?" she asked again, but made sure that every word pronounced was deliberately slow.

"As you can tell, I am not!" the girl retorted, her voice raised a little louder than normal.

"If you're not, then you'd kindly pull your skirt over your thighs, or I'll have to ask your parents to send you there! That includes all you young ladies, not just her!" our Geography teacher scolded, writing THIGH LAND in capitals on the blackboard.

Everyone's brows cleared and we laughed when we realized she was making up a fictious name and not referring to the country. A mischievous grin flitted across the girl's face, but she did as she was told.

When the bell rang signaling the end of the class, the girl grinned and said, "I like her. She cares about us." I was on the fence about that, though I was amused with the incident.

The reason why I wasn't in full agreement was because I once had an encounter with her that I didn't appreciate. I didn't like how she forcefully rubbed the unicorn's and my eyes when we were a few years younger, just because she thought we were wearing kajal to school.

She couldn't believe it was natural, even though we kept telling her we had thick lashes, and after she had satisfied herself that we were telling the truth, she didn't apologize for her rudeness.

She had a reputation for being quite a bully with the students and being partial to a few.

Some people mean well but often got in their own way

Every other day I was called by one of the unicorn's teachers because she was known as Miss Talkative. I didn't understand why I was being made responsible for telling the dragon and mermaid about it. Sometimes I didn't tell them because I didn't think the teachers needed to be so harsh. She was so little.

I also tried to tell the dolphin's bully to leave her alone, but I was instead called out for it and slapped by her class teacher who berated me in front of that bully who was equally shocked at the teacher's actions. From that day onward, the bully left my dolphin alone but her class teacher did not let her forget it.

Was this when I became the third parent? Nobody asked me to take on this role. I felt it take over and I did not know how to leave it behind.

A need to protect and defend my family became my navigating compass

Slingshots and paper messages were a normal pastime in my class.

I still can't explain why, but I found immense satisfaction in tracing the outline of my left hand on a piece of paper and decorating it during class. Maybe it was the simplicity of the task or the feeling of creating something unique. Whatever the reason, I was fully absorbed in my hand-art when suddenly, a tiny, folded piece of paper hit me.

At first, I thought it was a piece of chalk thrown by the class teacher, but as I felt its weight, I realized it was something else entirely. One of the backbenchers had carefully aimed a tiny paper projectile at me, slipping it through the rubber band slingshot she had crafted. The note inside read, "We're going to sit near the basketball court today."

However, I soon realized I wasn't the intended recipient. I was just a few inches off-target. I couldn't help but chuckle when I saw the name on the note and handed it to my neighbor, who seemed surprised. She was someone who enjoyed talking to me in class but would inexplicably ignore me outside of it. I found this behavior both silly and petty, and at the same time, I felt too old for such childish games.

**I could take myself somewhere else
when I was in the presence of people who couldn't see me**

My classmates didn't think I was interesting enough. I couldn't bear it. It hurt so much understanding this on some level, but my voice had always been so soft.

I couldn't be heard even when I tried to voice things I wanted to say. I wanted to change things, but I didn't know how and children can be cruel when they see that you want them to care.

I was invisible.

I liked my invisibility a lot,
but I would've given it up in a heartbeat for a true friend

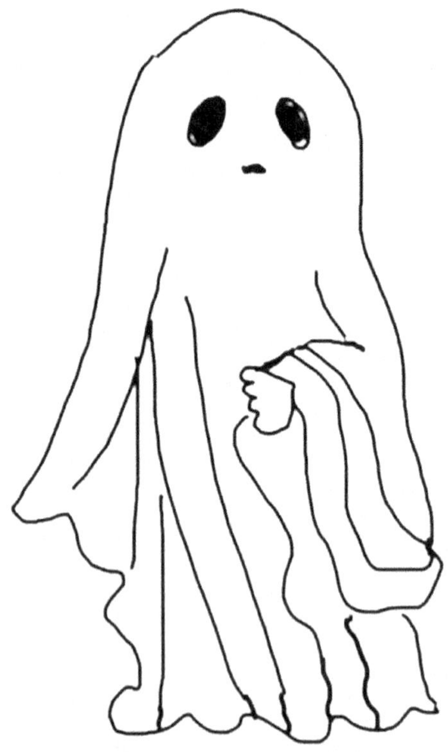

Several of my classmates had major crushes and would talk about them incessantly. I wondered why I couldn't relate to these emotions that they seemed to feel so strongly.

I liked and disliked men. It's intriguing that I somehow did not categorize the One into this. It always felt like he would not be like the rest because he would be all mine.

But I also wanted to fit in because now my classmates seemed to like me so I tried to smile and giggle at everything, desperately trying to be a part of it, wondering if anyone felt the way I did.

Women are complicated, but I guess we've practiced from a pretty young age

I loved to sketch.

I enjoyed gifting people my art, especially if I had been a recipient of their kindness. A girl in my 8th grade had been especially kind to me, so I naively drew her a picture and innocently asked if she liked me too.

Mayhem erupted. Gossip spread. I got caught in its spitefulness.

Classmates whom I had grown up with all these years started to steer clear of me. I later found out why from a classmate who hesitantly told me what the others were saying behind my back.

I was being called a lesbian and I felt sick to my stomach, thinking they had called me a bad word. I did not know what it meant until the mermaid explained it.

I didn't get it. I liked boys, didn't I? I wanted to marry a boy not a girl. But I also didn't want a bad man. I wanted a prince like the one the dragon had told me about.

Was admitting you liked and appreciated the kindness of someone wrong if you were the same sex? Why was it being misconstrued? This was all so ridiculously dramatic. I felt confused and more alone than before. I learned to be more guarded and to control my affection.

Later in life, I thought about those children who were gay. I cannot imagine the agony, struggles, and ostracizing they might have had to go through on their own.

My sensitivity to others' pain developed in a stronger way.

These were such tough lessons to experience.

Evil knows how to tear us down but we must keep on being kind

I was born without an arch in my feet, so doctors prescribed special sandals.

They hurt to walk in, but I'm unsure if I outgrew them or simply refused to wear them—probably the latter, given my stubbornness. As I grew, I didn't enjoy sports, possibly to also impress the mermaid. I would share every detail of my day with her and the unicorn would grow frustrated waiting for me to play. She'd ask, "Why do you have to tell the mermaid everything?" Her wisdom exceeded her age. Later, the dolphin took on this role, which I gradually left behind in my late teens.

My foot condition went unmentioned to teachers, who assumed I was fine. I found solace in the poetry of the hibiscus flower, abundantly growing everywhere in my school's gardens. I loved collecting their fallen blooms and felt a deeper connection upon learning that it was also called the "shoe flower." Discovering its uses in ancient tea, shoe polish, and makeup in several continents fascinated me.

As I delved deeper into the Bible, I found the *rose of Sharon* in *Songs of Songs* refers to the hibiscus, symbolizing resilience amidst thorns, comparing it to the likeness of being *the lily of the valleys.* This deepened my bond with the Weaver as I saw how He spoke to me in my love language by directly showing me His support towards my dreams. Someday, I'll marry *the apple tree from the forest*—the one who brings me comfort, shade, and fruit.

I thought I had big feet until I grew to my full height. Perhaps it was because amongst the unicorn and dolphin, it always seemed like mine were bigger. I still have only a slight arch.

Perhaps I am more human than I realized

"You're 5'1", my gym instructor said.

"Will I grow any taller?" I asked, still on the stand. We were getting our height reading done. I didn't like the thought of being in the first row forever.

"Probably about an inch or two", he confirmed as he passed his hand slowly but slyly over my chest, almost casually, like it was nothing.

I sighed, resigned.

I grew half an inch taller; I tell everyone I'm 5'2 though

I dreaded sports like the way the leaves dreaded Autumn. They knew they were going to fall.

My non-arched feet made it hard to run fast. I also had bad PE instructors in my primary years.

One made me run barefoot because I had accidentally worn the wrong shoes.

Another made me run laps across the long field because I was not fast enough.

"Slow coach", one PE instructor said in front of my class and made my classmates repeat it so I could feel ashamed along with another girl who stood with me. But the abuse didn't stop there. I was ostracized for being weak and left out of games with other kids. I started to feel like I was not good enough and I hurt in places already too hurt to recover.

Mental blocks began to form and I found myself making excuses, disliking sports with a passion, and dissolving slowly from within into visible nothingness.

I cannot understand how this type of abuse was allowed and accepted as normal

I started wearing humongous sweaters as I grew more conscious of my developing body. I tried very hard to flatten my chest, but sweaters were the best bet to remain unnoticed.

A suspicious teacher questioned my wearing of these sweaters in summer in front of the dragon and mermaid, but I just smiled and told them I felt safe from the cold.

They shrugged it off as a body temperature thing.

Nothing was normal, but I pretended that everything was

I hated school. I don't know why particularly.

Perhaps it's because I felt misunderstood, lonely, and invisible most of the time.

It felt like walking into a courtroom with the jury comprising of only the popular girls.

Chin up! I would tell myself. You've only a couple more years to go.

The red ink in my pen never stopped bleeding its truth

Since I got rejected by a few, I sat alone, unnoticed. They were not deliberately unkind, but it existed behind their cold logic. They just casually explained that I didn't bring importance to their cliques. I was not good in studies or in sports, nor was I cool.

I found myself walking to the chapel in anger. There, I stared at the big crucifix, sat down and screamed silently at the Weaver.

I raged and questioned Him.

Why couldn't anyone see me?
Why was I so damaged already?
What was wrong with me?
Why did He make me?
How could He be so unkind?

But all I heard through my tears was an odd, listening silence.

I started going there every day to have lunch with Him. Slowly, my anger began to die away as my conversation developed from a monologue of self-pity to a dialogue that enhanced my growth.

When I asked the Weaver for a loyal friend, he showed me Jesus; the Sun who I had been talking to all along.

The mermaid had told me that if I wanted a best friend, I had to be one. Now, I understood what she'd meant.

The Sun is the only friend I uphold above all others.

**When you know the quality of the friendship you bring,
you won't settle for superficial ones**

I needed the dragon to pick us up immediately or I would get abnormally anxious if he was even a little late.

I would constantly worry about where the unicorn and dolphin were. I didn't want to lose sight of them, so I would tell them to remain close until the dragon came.

I didn't like waiting for too long.

I started to forget how to be a child and sister

There was a lot of speculation in school about where babies came from. One girl said it happened when people slept naked together. She was the most accurate, but we thought that was a silly explanation and laughed at her, thinking it was just too disgusting for us to even imagine.

Didn't the dragon and mermaid teach us to cover ourselves and not let anyone see our bodies?

Another said babies were dropped by storks. Since we had all seen this on Cartoon Network, that made perfect sense.

But another girl said that if parents prayed and climbed up to the top of a hill, the Weaver would come in a helicopter and give them one or two or more babies if their prayers were strong enough.

I went back home and asked the mermaid to confirm these theories and she said the Weaver put them in her tummy. I tried to ask how, but she looked embarrassed and promised to tell me when I was old enough to understand.

I shrugged, dismissing it.

I preferred the story of the Weaver in a helicopter landing on a hill anyway.

I wish the generation before us weren't taught to be secretive about the most beautiful act created by the Weaver himself

I did not go anywhere without my trusty blue art notebook.

I loved carrying it everywhere I went. Sketching people was a passion of mine, and I found joy in capturing their likenesses and expressions on paper. At school, I loved it when my friends would notice my artwork and ask me to explain its meaning. Their curiosity would spark a sense of pride and enthusiasm in me, and I would happily dive into the stories and inspiration behind each piece.

Those moments were special, as they allowed me to share my creative vision and connect with my friends on a deeper level. It was a simple pleasure, but one that brought me great happiness and encouragement to continue exploring my artistic side.

Everyone knew I was an artist, not a writer

I had a soft corner in my heart for two classmates. We made up this silly game where they were the crows and I was the farmer because I wasn't as fast as they were.

I found that kindness could exist in the midst of loneliness and concealed trauma.

I'll always remember them for that.

Healing feels like the morning dew that falls after the night has been too dark

The Good Shepherd campus was vast in my childhood memories, comprising four schools, excluding the nursery.

Three of these schools were all-girls, with classes from Jr. 1 to 10th grade. We were identified by our ribbons or headbands—red, black, and white. White was my school's color. My uniform consisted of a dark brown skirt with thin maroon and white stripes for our shirts.

I remember the enchanting sound of a grand piano coming from the dusty red brick building opposite the nursery, close to the buildings where the red-ribboned girls from *St. Agnes'* school attended. One day, I saw a friend enter the building, and I curiously peeped in through the window to see what she was doing. A woman played beautiful music on the grand piano, while my classmate tried to follow on a Yamaha. Although she looked focused, she didn't seem to enjoy the lesson. The next day, I asked her if she took piano classes, and when she said yes, I eagerly asked if I could too. She shared the cost, and my eyes widened—it was impossible for me. I told the dragon and mermaid and I saw the sadness in their eyes. They told me that they wished they could afford it. My heart felt sad, but my spirit didn't give up.

The only other place I had access to a grand piano was at the dragon's oldest sister's home. She let me play, and I pretended to know how, even though I didn't. Later, when the mermaid's sister's family migrated, they left behind an electric Yamaha. I didn't know how to play expertly, but I studied the keys and learned to play my favorite musical themes years later, thanks to YouTube creators. Although no one nurtured this interest, I keep it close to my heart.

Hold on to every dream, and if it's good for your soul, the Weaver will provide the way

Reena Doss

It was in middle school that I finally found teachers I could look up to.

But I didn't fit in with my classmates. I tried to have conversations with the girls sitting beside me but I couldn't.

I wanted to talk about things that mattered, but they only wanted to talk about boys. I didn't think I liked boys and because I said so, they considered me too immature. I thought this was so ridiculous and I wanted none of it because every time a boy passed by, these girls would scream or act like noisy peahens who had spotted a peacock.

Please... give me a book any day.

Girls were as crazy as boys. Maybe there was something wrong with me?

I loved the library in school.

It was the only place I didn't feel so odd. Everyone had to be quiet, but that was perfect for me. It was my normal plus the bonus was—Books. I could go anywhere inside their stories.

I already loved to read, but I became a voracious reader as I discovered new words and gobbled them all up. My only regret was not using them to practice talking with people because speaking was not something I actively did back then, except at home.

But right at that moment in time, it didn't matter, having made the greatest discovery of my life. I had found a place where I could visit worlds that let me live in freedom and safety.

**Books understood me; they had so much
honor, integrity, adventure, beauty, and love**

My class teacher, Mrs. Bala, was worried about me. She asked me why I was unusually quiet and reserved. I wasn't able to come up with any explanation because I didn't understand myself at the time.

I had no clue how perceptive she was until we had the dreaded parent-teacher meeting. Surprisingly, she was the only teacher who had nothing disapproving to say. She complimented them on how well-mannered I was and asked the dragon and mermaid why I was so closed off from everyone. When they told her about how different I was at home, she was genuinely surprised.

Soon after that meeting, she set about taking a serious interest in my growth and asked me what I liked to do. When she found out I liked books, she made sure I had a lot of responsibilities in the library and continuously encouraged me to read.

She's someone I would like to meet again, just to tell her what a big difference she made in my life.

**There are people that the Weaver sends unexpectedly
who can change your life's direction completely**

Because of my class teacher, I started reading during assembly hours, rather than pretending to be too sick to go on stage. Another English teacher enjoyed my oration, so she would generally ask me to read in class.

I grew bolder as I began to give introductions to readings at Church. I found the courage to take part in a singing competition in front of the entire school. I sang *Memories* by Barbra Streisand and won third place because at some point, I got a little nervous and missed a stanza.

I was also selected to participate in an elocution for my house team—*St Lucy's*. I had randomly picked an article essay from a *Reader's Digest* (I loved reading these along with *Chicken Soup For The Soul*) called—*To Say I Love You*. I liked the story a lot because it was about how using the letter "e" simply or generously could convey the words themselves. I forgot the author's name but I do remember it starting with an "L". My new friend (who had bullied me when I was younger) was the one who spent many hours patiently listening and helping me perfect my chosen narration.

I won first place.

Kindness sparks a revolution, transforming into wings of freedom that let you be all you can be

Our class teacher had us organize and prepare an outreach program for an orphanage we were going to visit on Christmas Eve.

I will not forget those little faces filled with courage, starved of humanity yet so full of it themselves, who offered so much love while we took what we had for granted.

My classmates had discovered that I had a good voice and they asked if I would sing for the children. I nodded and even though I felt very shy, I sang because I knew it would bring them happiness.

My class teacher was so proud. I knew it was because she had believed in me.

I went home and asked the mermaid (at this point, it had become a heart desire) if we could adopt a few children. She said it wasn't possible and I wondered why because I knew we had a lot of love to give.

"Lord, when I get married, will you let us adopt orphans too? Amen."

**I've carried this desire in my heart since then
so I am not sure what the Weaver intends to do with it**

By this time, I had forged a very good friendship with three girls in school.

I lost touch with two of them, but they will always hold a very special place in my heart because when I felt utterly rejected and at my lowest, they were the only ones who reached out.

Despite us growing apart in our college days, the third girl is and will always be my friend. Her daughters are the loveliest dewdrops in the world.

30+ years of friendship. This friend is fine wine.

Hearts of gold are forged in ice, blood, fire, tears, and prayers

I was gifted Lassie by the swan when I turned 14. She was less than a month old but I'd seen her when she was just a week old—a ball of soft, black fur.

After that, the swan and I grew apart. I didn't understand why. We still talked, but we stopped hanging out like before. Perhaps it was because we missed another friend of ours that had to leave to another school. Before the fresh term began, we let our friendship fade even though we always talked after school while waiting to go home. I guess we both handled grief in our own way.

Lassie was a friend unlike any other, a counselor. She was like the therapist I never had and the only one who didn't take my barks seriously. I couldn't believe she was a German Shepherd with just 11 years allotted to her. I hope I get to see her again.

Is there a place for dogs in Heaven? I think there is.

I've asked many people, but no one seems to know. The dragon and the mermaid said they don't have a soul. "How do you know?" I asked. They looked confused and repeated what they were told. It didn't ring true to me. That's when I realized they didn't know.

I thought about this dilemma long and hard. Our first ancestors were the ones who upset the balance of Eden and that's why God had to make things right again for all of us to return. So maybe dogs and other living beings did go to Heaven, simply because they were not humans.

"Do dogs have a soul, Jesus?" I asked. There was only a calm silence but somehow, I found myself smiling. What a beautiful way to answer an overthinking child like me.

Strangely enough, the swan came back to find me a few months after Lassie passed away.

I still miss you, Lassie

The swan and I cherished our time together.

We often sat side by side during lunch breaks or after school, sharing stories and secrets. We'd exchange art, offer comfort, and advice when faced with challenges in school. Her creativity, deep thinking, and unique imagination inspired me, and I vividly remember the tales we'd concoct to entertain each other.

One story stands out in particular—a horror tale she'd retold, based on a movie she claimed to have seen. Her embellishments and vivid descriptions transported me to the scene, leaving me deliciously freaked out. I couldn't wait to share it with the unicorn and dolphin, who were equally captivated by the terrifying narrative. Years later, we discovered that the movie was a gothic comedy—*Dracula: Dead and Loving It*. We burst into laughter, amused by our childhood gullibility.

However, when the swan and I reconnected in 2011, we recalled those moments with a sense of nostalgia. Instead of laughter, we sat in symbolic silence, paying homage to our childhood selves and pondering who we had become in the present. It was a poignant moment, a testament to the power of friendship and shared memories that helped us find its threads with time.

Some year gaps can disappear like magic when your hearts are deeply connected

Not having a computer was a great disadvantage from the 8th grade onward as I was unable to catch up to the research levels of the other girls.

I fondly remember shocking the toppers in 5th grade when I once aced my *Computer Science* paper because they had long since decided that I was not up to their standards.

I loved *Computer Science* but was not allowed to take it in 8th grade because I had scored just below the required point. I was frustrated and upset. I'd wanted to learn programming because I felt it would help me in the future.

I had to take *Economics.* However, this turned out to be an advantage because along with the awareness gained from Social Studies, I learned necessary skills that would give me a leverage when I started college, joined university, worked in the corporate world, became a publisher and moved towards my dream of authoring my books.

I self-taught myself digital art later on in life.

The Weaver is very good at what He does.

The past becomes the perfect bridge when one can decipher its secret code of preparation in the present

One day, while sketching near the computer room, a senior student approached me and noticed my artwork.

She kindly offered to lend me her multi-color pen, and I was amazed by its vibrant hues and versatility. I felt like I had stumbled upon a magical tool, bringing my creations to life in a way I did not think possible. As I finished my art piece, I insisted on gifting it to her as a token of gratitude. She was deeply moved by the gesture, and we struck up a conversation, discovering a shared passion for reading.

Our chance encounter blossomed into a mutually admiring friendship, albeit short-lived, as she graduated that year, leaving me with two more years to go. Though our time together was brief, the memory of her kindness and our shared love for art and literature stayed with me.

**Sometimes, it is strangers who remind us of our gifts
more than those who surround us**

We finally had a coed inter-school event.

I met boys who seemed interested in me. I remember wanting to say something witty, but a weird thing would happen. Fear would paralyze me and something would steal my voice and I found myself very often tongue-tied.

It wasn't only because I felt shy, I kept choking on the memories of being touched the wrong way.

It did not deter them and I was unused to the attention.

A uniform can't conceal what makes you stand out

We did not have proms like they advertised in so many movies in the western world. We had what we called *The Socials*. It was basically a fancy term for a big tea party where we were allowed to dress up as long as we didn't show too much skin.

I remember my classmates begging the teachers to let them invite the all-boys school (opposite ours) to join us. I didn't mind the boys coming over this time because I had learned how nice it felt to be appreciated and get compliments, even though I did keep them at a distance. I was very curious about them too. But they were not allowed to come. Our principal was quite adamant about that.

It was not a big affair, to be honest. We were allowed to use the large hall for this function. We could play "loud" music as long as it was not too loud. Alcohol was forbidden, but we all acted like we were drunk on the soft drinks because this was the only day the entire staff was indulgent toward our craziness.

The teachers who had complained about us being the worst class in their history of teaching were now shedding tears and calling us the best class they had ever had.

They were a sentimental bunch, but I loved them all.

The end of a chapter should always be celebrated

Exams were a tedious affair.

I'd make last-minute lists, wondering why I'd postponed studying. Despite this, I'd manage to retain enough information to write my papers. Each year, we had more subjects, and the books seemed to grow exponentially. My brain felt like it had developed a mountain range inside. I tried not to let these changes affect me, but I noticed my classmates forming cliques based on societal norms. There were the high achievers, the popular ones, and the misfits—the creatives, dreamers, and those who struggled. I identified with the latter. However, there were exceptions in every group, and I remember the kind ones who were always willing to help.

One thing I hated was when office staff would announce late fee payments in front of the class, calling out names and implying that those who were late or made monthly payments weren't well-off. This would lead to smirks from my classmates, and I'd feel embarrassed. I told the dragon and mermaid, who didn't like this practice but felt powerless.

Before exams, we'd gather outside the hall, exchange tips, and wish each other luck. The invigilators seemed strict and bored, only focused on starting and stopping the clock. Exams could last up to three hours, with only a bottle of water allowed. If you needed to use the restroom, it was a torment, as some invigilators wouldn't let you go.

The agony didn't end there. At home, the dragon would scrutinize my paper, questioning every answer. The unicorn would claim to have lost her paper, which might have been a better strategy.

Then, teachers would announce each student's marks in class, which I thought was cruel. It puts undue pressure on a child's self-worth, intelligence, and capabilities.

The inner beauty of who we choose to be starts at a young age

I passed my ICSE boards.

No one could have been more stunned than I was. Not only that, I had achieved a second class. It wasn't something to be proud of, but to me, it was huge.

It was a victory I did not take lightly.

Curiosity and new goals like shaking hands with adversity

Everyone got emotional as we suddenly noticed friendships that could have existed if one had taken the time to try.

When we dressed up for *Graduation Day,* we wore the colors of the rainbow. A few of us weren't too happy with the bright, vibrant shades, but we went along with the majority of raised hands.

My saree had a Spanish rose tint and its satin glimmered as we walked the aisle toward the stage, holding our candles and singing *I Believe I Can Fly.* The pride on the dragon and mermaid's faces as they stood up to watch us go past them made up for any misgivings or foolish anxieties I might have had about fashion.

I was thrilled when Grandy attended my graduation too, along with my godmother and the dragon's oldest sibling. I was asked to pose in pictures from classmates who rarely spoke to me.

At the end of our graduation ceremony, the sober reality proved to be a shocking reminder that this particular stage in life was over.

Cameras kept clicking. When did I become popular?

We were going on a class trip to Coorg. It was exciting.

The dragon and mermaid made sure that we did not miss any annual school trips. I will forever be appreciative of this gift because I know it was not easy for them.

Only final year students were allowed to go for these two-day excursions with our class teachers and Principal. I was so happy I could go.

We did so many things together, including seeing a reserved Tibetan village, saw a beautiful waterfall, stayed in hotel, acted like lunatics singing like crazy in the bus and stressed out the staff that were in charge of us. It was the only time I remembered feeling like I was a part of my class. Some even expressed the surprising wish that they should have spent time hanging out with me. I thought this was very sweet of them and told them so because I know they genuinely meant it.

Change restructures perception and transforms old eyes

During a holiday visit to Chennai, the unicorn, dolphin, and I met the mermaid's cousin's son, who had a type of muscular dystrophy. Despite his condition, he was the funniest and jovial person I'd ever met.

Unfortunately, many people lack awareness about how muscular dystrophy affects the body and nervous system. He used a wheelchair, but his spirit remained unbroken. His mother was his rock, yet she credited him for giving her strength. He was incredibly intelligent and loved playing games with us, but what struck me was his fondness for holding the remote control—a childish quirk that reminded me of the unicorn, dolphin and I. When it was time for us to leave, he was devastated, and his mother comforted him as he cried.

Tragically, the next news we heard was of his passing. This experience prompted me to learn more about muscular dystrophy, its various types, and how it can shorten one's lifespan. Though I don't know which type he had, his memory stays with me.

**The fragility of life should teach us
to hold on to what love is even more**

A house has not represented security for me.

Before my 15th year, we had lived in ten different homes, including temporary stays with relatives during transitions between rented places. I felt like we were constantly on the run, chasing unfulfilled dreams rather than embracing the future's possibilities.

Perhaps this is when I internalized the undercurrents of sadness, providing a refuge for it to reside within me. Maybe this is when I adopted survival as my primary goal, with failure becoming a familiar and comfortable companion. Possibly, this is when I began navigating the shadows of a past that lingered in my bones like an echo, unknowingly building a home for it within myself.

What else had I inherited on this nomadic journey?

Monkeys have made visits to our homes, especially the two in Egipura.

There were huge open spaces near these two houses in this particular town. It was part of the less populated suburban regions of Bangalore, and that is why glimpses of snakes and monkeys were not at all uncommon guests.

The first encounter occurred when the dolphin was still crawling. From the top layers of trees near our terrace, a big monkey slid onto our balcony. The dolphin sat near the front door, happily munching on a banana. I spotted the monkey first from my seat on a mattress in the hall and alerted the mermaid. Startled by my reaction and the monkey's sudden presence, the dolphin threw her banana and screamed. The suave monkey picked it up, eyeing the dolphin with a puzzled expression, and began advancing. I feared he might grab her, but the mermaid arrived just in time having heard the dolphin crying.

The monkey was startled, but the mermaid's intimidating posture didn't faze him. Clearly, he had dealt with mama monkeys before but wasn't in the mood to take on a human one. He clutched the banana tighter, anticipating she might take it and decided to leave. As casually as he had appeared, the monkey climbed back onto the balcony and exited without haste. We breathed a sigh of relief and laughed at the absurdity of the whole episode.

Another time, from our terrace, we witnessed a poignant reunion. A lone baby monkey swung from tree to tree, calling out for his family. The dragon speculated that he'd been left behind, and the mermaid concurred, but she was confident his mother would return. And return she did. After two hours of the little one's plaintive cries, a large monkey arrived, but the baby refused to budge until his mother appeared.

With agile grace, she navigated the branches, coaxing him down from his lofty perch. Initially hesitant, the baby monkey eventually descended and reunited with his mother. Their reunion was heartwarming—a warm hug, followed by a stern spanking, teaching him a valuable lesson. We couldn't help but chuckle. Once his hunger was sated, his mother effortlessly hoisted him onto her back, ready to depart. But then, a remarkable display of leadership unfolded.

The big monkey, clearly the leader, waited patiently for the mother and baby to join the group. Only when everyone was accounted for did he lead the troop forward, ensuring that all were safe and ready.

The third encounter occurred at the house where a snake had once entered. Lassie, then just eight months old, cherished the spacious garden, racing wildly from end to end, ferociously guarding her territory despite her gentle nature.

One day, as monkey families passed through, Lassie chased them. As she leaped against the wall, a massive monkey grabbed her neck scruff and slapped her with his other paw. Stunned, Lassie ceased barking and attempted to nip his grip, but the monkey adeptly shifted his hold, slapping her again. He repeated this, mocking her attempts. But the monkey's actions weren't malicious; he was simply protecting his community. He seemed to sense that she was still a pup and so his slaps were more in the form of correction rather than trying to seriously maim her. Once the other monkeys crossed the wall, he released Lassie and bounded over the wall himself.

We were relieved to find Lassie furious but unharmed. She refused to come inside the house until she was convinced the monkeys were far away. Afterward, we kept a close watch for monkeys, ensuring Lassie stayed indoors.

**In the delicate dance between humans and wildlife,
may we step forward with compassion for all living beings**

When we got a telephone, I was already 13.

The mermaid had also stopped writing letters and people stopped sending cards. The mobile phone had already been making its entrance into our side of the world by this time. Previously, I remember seeing rotary dial telephones in every home I visited and their circular faces were a familiar sight so I was excited to discover that our first and new telephone didn't have a rotary dial, but instead featured a sleeker design and an answering machine. We were all thrilled to have it in our home and eagerly set it up with the help of our eldest cousin brother from the dragon's side.

He patiently answered our numerous questions, chuckling at our enthusiasm as we explored the phone's features. As we recorded our voices for the answering machine, he offered guidance and encouragement, happy to see us so excited about this new addition to our home. Once we were all set, he left us to enjoy our new phone, and we spent hours touching and admiring it.

The ways of communication have evolved so quickly yet distance can still be agony

The mermaid's two cousin brothers from Malaysia visited us and quickly took a liking to the unicorn, dolphin, and me.

They bombarded us with questions, and when they arrived to take us out for dinner, they noticed my art portraits, which I had forgotten were on display between the glass showcase's sliding doors. One of them asked the mermaid who the artist was, and when she revealed it was me, he eagerly asked about my inspirations, why I focused on painting faces, and my future aspirations. He praised my bold, colorful, and confident strokes, and even asked if I had any fashion design ideas, as his wife worked in the industry. I blushed and beamed, feeling a bit tongue-tied, but managed to express my gratitude.

We enjoyed a pleasant dinner, and I appreciated their company. One brother was quiet and observant, while the other was playful and fun-loving. Before departing, they reiterated their offer to support me if I pursued the fashion line. I thanked them for their generous offer but I was torn between doubt about my abilities and what the dragon and mermaid thought about it. When I shared my fears with the mermaid, she said that I didn't have to pursue it if I wasn't interested in it. Yet, I was but I didn't say so. I got quiet instead.

I couldn't shake off the feeling that something was holding me back. I couldn't pinpoint what it was except that something dark was moving between the folds of my path and I felt blindfolded. I was experiencing a lot of internal changes as well as noticing things around me shifting. I was drowning in something deeply uncertain. But even as I tried to uncover what it was, it remained elusive.

When deep waters choose shallow living, life becomes a challenging journey

I attended my first youth pilgrimage.

We went to Goa and I received a Word by chance. I saved the bookmark that I got along with that reading.

I received my second random proposal but then I told him my age. That, along with the fact that my older cousin brother and my uncle—who was a priest—were in that same group, probably changed his mind. I felt sorry for him for how could he have known? But then again, who goes around proposing to someone they'd just met?

I could not see the significance of the Word I received until later on in life. It was a Word so powerful; it knocks me to my knees just reading it today, shocking me with its hope and saving power.

I was being pushed forward in a new direction and I started to notice how the Weaver's presence affected everything from that point on.

**Conversations with the Weaver deepened to an intimacy
that I have not experienced with another soul**

I wanted to join a Catholic Pre-University college because I knew there would be opportunities to grow my faith. I had my heart set on one in particular as it was known to be one of the top colleges in Bangalore and I wanted to be able to pursue my Bachelor's degree there as well.

It was nearly impossible to get selected because they required first class results. It was a slim chance and a risk because I had applied to only two colleges.

I prayed that if I didn't get into the college of my choice, I would at least be accepted into the second one.

I didn't think about what would happen if I didn't get selected.

I couldn't afford to.

Competition is a fierce thing and I had grown used to being swallowed up by the wild

I hoped that the times of being unnoticed would finally be over and that good times were indeed coming. When we went to check the results, I was too afraid to look.

When the dragon called out to me in excitement, I did not expect to see what I saw—my name.

There it stood; proud, placed along with a list of top students. I thought the college had made a mistake. I was probably the only one with a second class who was chosen. I broke down, crying in gratitude.

I got accepted into the other college too.

I was in shock for a long time after that because I knew with a certainty that the Weaver had some plans in store for me, but I was going to have to work very hard and leave the rest to Him.

I knew the Weaver had not judged my marks card, but had judged my heart and weighed its desire to make a difference in the world. I thanked him with all my heart for believing in me.

The Weaver's love is consistently unconditional

No way was I going to take Hindi again. I had a huge mental block about the language and based on my track record of trying to pass, I was terrified of feeling like a failure again.

The dragon, mermaid and I pleaded with the Vice Principal to let me take French. He considered my marks card carefully before turning to meet my eyes for a long moment.

"If I let you take French", he said, "I want your word that you will score above 80 percent".

"Yes, I promise," I said solemnly.

He looked at me again, then nodded, pleased.

He signed my request form to take French and I scored above 90 percent that first year. He was the first principal who ever believed in me. I did not want to let him down.

My word meant everything to me because it was all I had

I had been struggling in some subjects, unsure of what was wrong.

Some classmates found it irritating when I asked to borrow their books to copy notes I couldn't keep up with. A few kind ones let me copy their notes during break times. I would improve at note-taking when I sat closer to the blackboard, feeling less embarrassed to ask for help. I told the dragon and mermaid I was struggling to see in class, but I didn't explain how it affected my well-being. I didn't want to seem weird wearing glasses, even though I knew I needed them.

It wasn't until I started pre-university that I got my first pair of glasses. The relief was immense, and the pressure behind my eyes disappeared. I could finally see clearly— the clock at home, bus numbers, store signs. I felt like I was wearing magic, and I was overjoyed.

Gone were the headaches and eye strain from reading. I no longer needed to ask for help with notes. It's astonishing how something so simple can change one's life trajectory. Now, others asked me for help and to copy my notes. I was happy to assist, knowing that kindness is remembered long after the deed becomes a part of time's fabric.

Love may reside within the soul but is only felt when we give it to others

The weirdest thing began to happen.

I could talk with complete ease to girls way older than me, yet I could not connect with anyone my age. They would start asking me for advice as they disclosed things they found difficult to speak to others about.

But what surprised me the most was my level of comfort in talking with those that were hurting and alone because I would find myself always willing to listen and help.

The moon began to use her gravity to submerge herself within the ocean's depth

One of the things I loved to do was mix languages so that the depth of my feelings could be found in the union of languages rather than a single one.

I think this habit of mine was formed when I used to be laughed at for not knowing my mother tongue, or punished in school for not getting it right, or even mocked for not knowing a language other than English—the one I breathed in and out through all my senses. These events didn't motivate me to learn another specific language in its entirety, and maybe that was a good thing. Because I love that I chose words from languages that were beautiful to me, words that seemed to play new music tones when I listened carefully, cupping my hands around my ears like shells.

By using the language I love and combining it with the languages of the world, I let my heart feel every word I use when I write for the love I know is for me. It gives me pure joy when I can be who I was created to be with him.

I am an Earthian, after all

I saw poetry in the world around me.

I peeled back its essence in nature. I found it in the gentle way a black ant carried a crumb I had dropped, working together with a fellow ant to store it for winter. What was just a crumb to me was a truckload of food to them.

I pondered how we often crush ants without a second thought, sometimes unintentionally, sometimes out of fear or when the red ones bite us. I also thought about those who did it just because they could and this made me contemplate the mentality of kindness and how it's not something that needs to be learned. There are many traits like this hiding behind people that can be noticed if you take the time to observe who they are before we bring them into our inner circles.

I felt emotions in images that revealed poetic lines, but I didn't know how to express them until writing became a necessity. Looking back at old notes and scribbles, I realized how poetic each piece was, but I only recognized this when my heart started its fight for survival.

Poetry was always a part of me, waiting to be uncovered

Ocean

School was over and my days as
a *Pearl on a Summer leaf*
had finally come to an end
Spring had glided into Summer
and Summer had melted into Fall
and before I knew it, I was
o u t   o f   m y   s h e l l

I felt less like myself
I didn't feel as complete anymore
Pieces were missing
I had been split right down the middle
I was terrified and uncertain
as I peered through the cracks
of my once whole Pearl-shaped egg

I knew that I had to grow and survive the test of time
before I was ready to welcome a new season again
I was only beginning…
How strange to be saying that at just 15

I breathed deeply
and took my first steps out
and into the water of sound

unknown

Would the waves streaming in hurt?

Reena Doss

We all exist on singular paths,
plurally aligned together, walking with each other.
-Leon, a quote from Travellers For Life
by Miriam Otto and Reena Doss

The Dragon

forgot his strength, size, and courage

Imagination stems from the nostrils of the dragon.

It seeps into the mischievous twinkling of his eyes and spreads into the maddest jokes he improvises.

The secret of his magic bursts forth from his core of hardships and trials wherein lies the legend; that of a dragon that only springs forth with joy when he finally realizes that his presence is acknowledged, his demons are banished into the realms of the past and his heart bursting with fire is loved.

There is great depth to his elemental dungeon of solitude but he guards his treasures fiercely, afraid of the craftiness, cruelty, and greed of humankind that he had experienced many times before.

Turbulent and suspicious of those that seek him out, he hides away in a prison of his own making, roaring fire on all who approach, making no distinction between predators and like-minded souls.

Unaware that the core of his existence depends upon his gifted visions and courage to pursue them, he contemplates the Creator's reasons for his purpose—uncertain of who he was, is, and who he will become.

Now grown older and wiser, he weaves tales out of sparks of fire and ash, entertaining the young and the old alike, awaiting the day of his salvation and rescue from the designated guise he'd been allotted from the beginning of time.

Reena Doss

Grandy Egypt

your eyes would light up when they saw me

Thank you for my creative and imaginative dragon.

Thank you for being there at every great teen event in my life and for encouraging and supporting me in my dreams, ventures and ideas and for not doubting in my success.

Thank you for softening your once known strictness so many times with me when I talked with you. You told me why when I asked why you acted in certain ways.

Your name has historical significance and a store of wealthy stories. Your life has been one exciting adventure that I enjoyed listening to as I grew, especially the ones about the dragon. You left behind a rich legacy of children, grandchildren and great grandchildren.

No matter what, I will remember you as a woman with an indomitable spirit. I'm glad I got to say goodbye to you and received your blessings before I left that year. May the Lord grant you eternal peace and may His loving perpetual light shine upon you forever.

And like I promised you, I will write a book based on some part of your life, most probably. the romantic story of how you and Grandpa met.

The Mermaid

was born to give life in three worlds

The mermaid has a wealth of knowledge that holds her captive under the surface but did not reveal much for fear of being discovered.

Her desire to belong on land has been paramount to even giving up exploring her truest passions that run through the water in her veins.

Regret sometimes haunts and steals her beauty until she reminds herself of her worth.

An allure of mysticism surrounds her crown of silver waves, lurks on the corner of her smile and under the edge of her sharp nose.

She will sacrifice her legs to let us smell love coming from the kitchen to darn ripped clothes, and listen for hours on end to every sad, boring or happy tale.

She will hide underwater, covering her own worries with an absent-minded frown as she watches us leave home on paths that might not always make sense to her with a whimsical light as she will look up at the sky, praying for our safe return.

She gets wistful after reading those unending dreams of lifetimes she could have lived in.

She wonders about the futility of choices and the design of the Creator, yet manages to find time to laugh and grow with us.

A rare creation, she can be incredibly brave, yet enormously shy as she tosses her moonlit hair and emerges from her life under the sunset ocean to witness the sunrise before the start of each day.

Reena Doss

Nana Agnes

you encouraged the heart of me

Night silk with moonlit eyes.
Eyes that devoured all she saw.
Saw that love was the keepsake of the heart.

Heart of gold embroiled in deep emotions.
Emotions that enveloped her many children.
Children with children that she sang songs.

Songs of the past that they together laughed about.
About strict parents who did normal things.
Things that had become extraordinary.

Extraordinary ears listened to their dreams.
Dreams of lives untold but boundless in imagination.
Imagination that was wistfully sky-high.

Sky-high, she watched over the landscape.
Landscape of her descendants as they flourished.
Flourished in the joyful knowing of her love.

Love that took secrets and stories to God in prayer.
Prayer that I make for her soul to eternally rest.
Rest in glorious peace, my beloved Nana.

Nana, how I long to see you again.
Again comes the visits of the night.

The Pyramid

little King, you live upon the most beautiful shores of my heart

I didn't always know he existed until I was older but when I found out one day that he was part of the womb we all shared my tears were inexplicable. I thought about the adventures, the conversations, the sibling drama and how nice it could have been to have had a brother growing up with us. How could I love, feel so deeply and grieve for my brother whom I did not know?

There is no grave or document that marks his arrival. I wonder if his Guardian Angel carried him the whole time he was here. I told him not to let it get to his head if I told him that I keep his memory in imaginary books for children within the best doors of my heart that I will open when I know it is time.

A heart has four chambers just like a pyramid has four sides. They hold the face to all sides of a compass and direct ships lost at sea to safe land. They can act as sun dials on the sand when everything on the land is parched, bruised and cracked. When the shadows fall, you will know where the setting of the night is taking place and where the rising of the Earth's star will begin.

David means beloved or favorite and I think that's perfect because my little brother was born to remind me that Heaven is real and waits for us. I know he adds prayers for the times we forget or can't or won't pray when we need to. Perhaps I will meet him in the life after this because the sting of death will not exist there. I realized then that he is a tomb within me that did not need a burial for the sun shines so brightly on the meaning of his very name.

I ask the Weaver why he wasn't allowed to stay sometimes. I ask the wrong questions I know because there are no answers for many things. But what I do sense is that my baby brother is in the safest hands and most importantly—he is happy and playing.

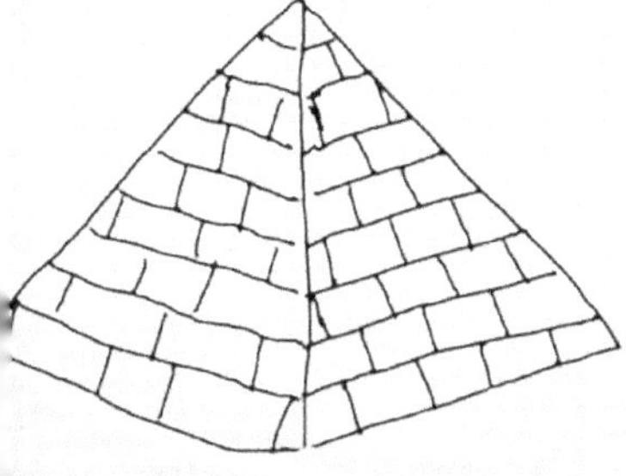

Butterfly

be all that you wish to be

Be a swan. Speak deep words of the ocean. You cannot drown here because you will sail to places where no one else can. Do not hide in waters where you can glide in. You must learn to speak the languages of the silent worlds beneath, beneath, beneath the storms of the seas.

Be a mermaid. Travel far and wide into the great unknown. Let the sleeping songs within you arise, arise, arise in the wake of the morn. Sailors will hear and come but let the winds of time steady you when you sit upon the rock that defines you.

Be you. You are not made for ordinary pens or brushes. Stories of you can breathe many worlds. They will stretch and grow beside you so let your wings expand and become.

You are worthy of the space you carve so fly, fly, fly, B U T T E R F L Y

Be all that you wish to be.

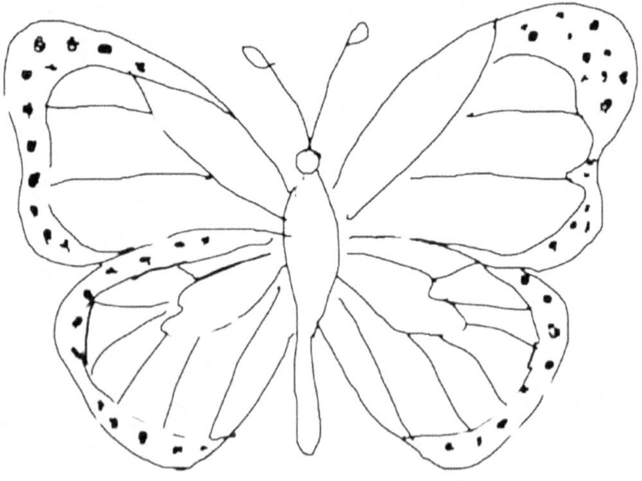

The Unicorn

must not be defined by its horn

She's a unicorn with the gift of wisdom to discern the past, interpret the present and logically assess the possible consequences of the future. She has that terrifying ability to look through you and see all that you are and still accept you.

I am constantly amazed by the evolution of magic she finds within to reshape her world from pointed edges to circular walls bridging broken sides by growing beautiful ivy and oak tree roots where enemies and friends somehow can coexist with each other through their respect and fascination in her abilities of wisdom and seeing powers.

If you cross paths with her, be assured that you will witness miracles. If she has chosen you to remain in her circle, it means you are infinitely precious. She will always see the good in people because she has that ability to be kind despite cruelty, to be generous in the midst of selfish greed, to glimpse the wonder of the midnight sky and to illuminate souls with her own special brand of magic.

Words are not enough for the languages learned in her heart; hence pay attention for she will speak with actions through her eyes, and in the gentle shyness that lies within her courage and boldness.

A few words of caution: Do not try to possess this mythical legend for though she considers herself a part of everyone she belongs to none for she will not accept being caged. To destroy the spirit of such purity of heart is a shame because her kind is rare and far between.

Listen for the clickety-clack of her heels under the sliver moon's shadows after dusk for she brings its radiant otherworldly light with her.

Reena Doss

Dragonfly

you have time

Be gentle with time.

You are an hourglass of the Sun, warm in the sunshine, fearful of the rain. You are dying and being born every day. Settle into the in-betweens of this sorrow you carry. It's okay not to be happy. It's okay to take the smile off. It's okay to be quiet on the outside.

Sometimes, laughter is a tale of sadness when the hurt can no longer be contained. Release the darkness from your eyes. I see the stars bursting from within. Drink from the oases in the desert. Rest under the shades of the trees. Grasshoppers flirt with the violins of spring but you are not like them.

You are a Dragonfly with translucent wings of black and gold, caught on the notes of a piano string that yearns to be free. Release your soul so your heart may find its voices. What passion and love you wield when you let your hands create joy.

There is no need to be at war… You have a storm that you do not know. Let it be who it is supposed to be. Let it arrive. Let it. Be gentle, little one, be gentle and the skies will fall at your feet.

You are from the deep and growth is what you need. You will rise with the seas.

You have time.

The Dolphin

always knows the way back home

She's got a heart made of sungold spun from the threads of starlight under a blue moon.

She races the surface of the changing waters, bursting with laughter at the rhythm of the world and twirling in circles underwater to bury her moods.

To make you find comedy in the day that she sees, she'll walk backwards on the edges of her tail, then swoop high in the air, spray water on everyone and clap her hands happily with helpless glee. Contagiously known to make the globe laugh, no one often understands the sad tales she hides out of sight.

She embarks on voyages unknown to the language of the common tongue, enthralled with the mystery of how things work beneath the surface of what is visible and dances with the sprites of mischievous light and redeeming hope.

She rescues melancholy souls with color in all her thoughtful ways but retreats into sullen despair when her open ways are betrayed by the sly ones who try to take advantage by pinning down her fins, but she will always find escape in ordinary chains that bind for they cannot tie her for long.

She will always be able to see what lies beneath the cold surface of whispered secrets softly uttered, well-modulated tones of speech and raging notes stuck beneath their shadowed masks. She will discern the offer of a fin that invites drowning souls to take hold of it in a rescue, leading them back to safer waters.

Sweet, fun-loving, and kind to all created works of nature, she is a painted dolphin, etched among the colors of blue, gray, and purest sunlight. To her belongs the secrets of the unseen for she was not made to belong to the world of sight.

Reena Doss

Firefly

love will always remain

You have travelled through so many changes of the heart.

Your mind is a dazzling garden that hasn't begun to sing.

May the paths you walk upon today be the stepping stones for the times when you will need to hop upon them while navigating through the restless seas within your soul. May your depth grow to become a poetic minefield of ready to explode yellow daffodils. May the creative feathers that you gift to others from your sweet wings be the seeds that will follow you when they blossom at the time you most need them. May you receive the joy that comes with every new chapter to fearlessly explore your purpose and to pursue it relentlessly, no matter the storms.

I hope you don't stop trying to shed all the layers that hold you back from your dreams. I hope you stay true to who you are as you walk on the path that calls to you. I hope you always dive into the unknown.

Be proud of yourself for finding your voice to speak up for what matters, for the spirit within you that always tries her best and for the love that always shines.

Always remember, you are important to me.

When everything is taken apart, love will always remain.

The Eagle

Its song will live on through the ages

I've wondered if one day I would sometimes fly o'er valleys and lakes and perhaps just perch up high on the topmost mountain of a kingdom that will be mine.

Hurrying by, ten thousand people jostle below, shoving each other to an odd little show. What a funny conundrum to watch this view—so elevated!

My prey, I soar and swoop to catch, grasping by hooked claw and beak. Tough to see, 'tis frightening. Necessary for survival, it is my right. For unlike the creatures of the human race who slaughter life like a game—a choice, I haven't. A voice, I have but still…

I dream of mountains high. How they can reach the sky; craggy rocks and briar roses, therein I'll build a home far away from the human race. A safe abode. A nest for my young. Protected, they must be from all types of heathen cruelty.

Those particular men who savagely take, steal and break. What isn't theirs is fun! They'll destroy us all for power and lust.

The young are touched in their home, alone. Innocence, quenched all at once. Fire burns those tender growing lights when rage buried, consumes.

The ache of the molested cannot be undone… It carries over every day. Suppressed hurt, a rotting grave.

No one has time to trust when it's been questioned before. Time and again, man's betrayal—ripples and ripples.

His voice, I hear in my heart. Fear resurrects. I watch and mock his falseness. Every gesture for the crowd. They cannot see, they cannot know. But how could they not see? They turn their eye and love his illusion.

A sniper's vision is my tool. I'll peck his eyes out if I could for no baby nest can feel secure.

My eggs will hatch to Earth's own song for if he comes near, with my telescopic lens, I'll protect my own.

A screech from up high, I'll call on the hawks of the night to rip him to shreds so he finally knows how to bleed inside my traumatized hell.

I want to go away from this toxic block.

Tall granite and cold stones.

So much smoke and dust...
An eagle on a cloud, am I.

I stay aloof and cast my eye.

Three

we are as different as can be

I slipped into the world on the bridge between Summer and Autumn. The one after me heralded life to bid the Winter months goodbye. The one after her brought in the welcoming birds of Spring as our parents freed lanterns into the night sky.

We are not about our mother's or father's tattoos and quills, though we all draw strength from the same blood ink. We are not made of borrowed paper-mâché gifted to us by kindly souls to wear. We are not all that the crickets chirp into your evening cup of gossip. We are laughter, tears, pain, and joy swirled into a champagne glass. We carry the wealth of the human spirit, the sweet labor of broken, creative hands and the bravery of tumultuous, forgotten hearts. We can design constellations and attract galaxies to bathe in our worlds. We paint stars, hold pixie dust and dreams as we dance under the sun filled with moonlight. We orbit each other on parallel paths and collide into our asteroids when we're down and want to drown. We can raise comets to feed you hope and cast a never-fading sun's love upon your hearth.

Block your ears from jealous lies and experience the tales passed on from the trusted and know from our voices that they are not often the truth you seek.

Ask us who we are directly and we'll tell you. Our hearts are open oceans; they are incomprehensible if you sit in a boat on its edge, afraid to dive in.

Come, discover our stories—we are beautiful, strong, and free. Let us take your hand so you can see that together—we are more, we are you, we are love and we will always be—three.

Reign Fire

I know how to fly into the flames

Let any fire reign down on me.

I am not afraid of speaking up. I am kind but fierce in my heart. I am not a doormat because I see your provocations and can be still if I chose but this time, I will not. I have a steel made backbone under the gentleness you see. Don't you know what is in my blood?

I conjure beauty in realms that others see as haunted. I spoke the language of the dolphin and unicorn from a young age to communicate to the rivers I grew up with. I inherited the dragon's rage to breathe, the mermaid's ability to disappear into herself but I have not used them in the same way because I had the wind to take me into my worlds of music, laughter, words, creativity and art.

I use my rage to champion things that matter in little ways, in the ways I exist. I use my art of disappearance to locate the source of pain to dance in the ink of my stories. All lurk beneath the surface and refuse to come out when they sense fear trying to read them without the boldness of belonging.

I take to the skies and dive into the waves and that is how I know I have wings, not heavy ones of legacy but born from the light I painted with the help of the sun and the phoenix colors that I dream in.

Mystical Rose

mother of the Morning Star and mine

There are unsung tales in the hearts of mothers. They bleed dark truths and shape our hopes. They believe in us when our buildings turn to rubble.

After we lay our broken hearts within the shelter of their arms, we find the strength to turn pain into progressive action. We begin to rebuild our collapsed foundations, and realize that tear-stained bricks are often the strongest ones needed to reclaim a home lost for many years occupied by too many opinions.

It is our mothers who clean the debris, so we can have a place of our own to recover from illusions, monsters and cruel setbacks. They leave us alone yet hold us close, letting walls fall upon them, uncaring of their own discomfort as they throw their bodies on the line again and again and again—to keep us safe from shaky restarts when we unintentionally strike out at them while striving to attain the impossible.

In dungeons we didn't know were built around us, where all light remains unseen and we lie trapped under fallen dreams, mothers step in to remind us that we are loved unconditionally, unreasonably, overwhelmingly by an ever present loving God waiting for the exact time to set our courage on fire—to become a rising flame to lift others like us from wallowing in the endless dark.

My mother's eyes carry galaxies of hope for tomorrow.

My mother's smile heals the past of countless sorrows.

My mother's arms overflow with an abundance of love.

I see it all in wonder and thus, I rise, I rise, I rise.

Reena Doss

Soul Footprints

will separate old roots and guide you to your own

Sometimes, I think that there are souls left behind in the footprints of my parents—souls that carry forgotten dreams of regret and an urging to fulfill them.

They toss and turn and embark on a daily mission to instill in me these long-held yesterdays as I seek their approval going about achieving these hopes.

These types of souls are not the kind that force but encourage me to build my dreams, yet always with the presence of a guided history of their own.

Unknown to me, tethering on the unconscious level, I create another soul of footprints for the coming generation.

I fill it to overflowing with my dreams that I shove aside regularly, determined to release into the boundless freedom these fading souls of my parents. Uncertain about the why, needing to assuage their hurt experienced over many lifelong years spilled, scattered, and then spread like jam on a toasted slice of bread that I eat and swallow, nodding my head in a state of coma, a slave to needing appreciation, all the time knowing that sugar is probably bad in the long run.

They cannot see what I don't allow myself to see. They do not feel what I am numbing myself with. They do not understand what I am trying to communicate.

Until I find the courage to release my soul, to sing its own music, with no excuse after knowing what it was born to do, they cannot see, feel or understand.

But these souls that exist inside my parents' footprints, slip and slide between each other, confusing my little feet trying desperately to keep up with a history I have not walked in before.

Life has been a great teacher, patient yet determined in its efforts to continuously wash them away as soon as I catch up, like what the waves swiftly do with my doodles on the shore…

I realize then that their paths are not mine to take.

I must find mine by using their faded steps as guidelines and at the same time, not darkening them through reruns.

Sometimes, I think I might be inclined to follow footprints not made by those of my parents to help influence and develop what I need to shape because I do not want to leave a soul of regret in them.

I want my future generation to try and create their own footprints, allowing mine to finish their life journey before getting eroded away in time, embraced daily by sand and water.

I must leave the souls of my parents to make their peace with the waves and shores. I must step into a road unmarked, a mystical path with adventures unknown, a silent trail without leftover instructions.

And yes, it is quite possible that I might leave behind a soul or two under the soles that I walk in. All I can hope for the ones who do step into them is to realize that they are not theirs.

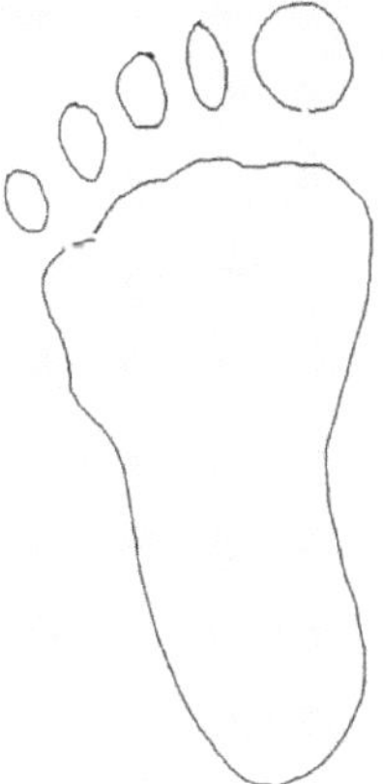

Your Purpose

is a lifetime mission

The ant felt frustrated and isolated, asking if there was a scam in the way she had been created within the Most High's perfect plan.

"Give me arms to carry the world," said the ant to the Most High.
"That's not your purpose", was His compassionate reply.

"Give me a mind that can change the world," said the ant to the Most High.
"That's not your purpose", was His gentle reply.

"Give me hands so I can touch the world," said the ant to the Most High.
"That's not your purpose", was His mischievous reply.

"Give me ears to listen to the world," said the ant to the Most High.
"That's not your purpose", was His laughing reply.

"Give me eyes to see the world," said the ant to the Most High.
"That's not your purpose" was His merciful reply.

"Give me wings to travel the world," said the ant to the Most High.
"That's not your purpose", was His still patient reply.

The ant wasn't deterred, though she let out a deep sigh:
"Lord, I'm as small as can be. My eyes can't see what you plan for me.
Life can be tough; I don't feel good enough. Ahead, the roads are rough.
I trudge all day long, singing the same song. This path I'm on seems wrong.
Can you please guide my heart? I've forgotten its allotted part
in my zeal to create magnificent art."

The Most High smiled at the ant and put forth a question:
"What seed does the world need to avoid its lust to feed greed?"

The ant thought about this for a while, then asked again, more sure of her reply:

"Lord, I've asked for many things through my ego and pride, but if you could give me anything, please give me a heart full of hope that cannot die, for the world needs its seed to eliminate its lust to feed greed."

"Ah, now that I can do, my dear little one", said the Most High,
"for your purpose has always been greater than you think.
I made you small so that the world can see
how greatness begins when you are free,
how big you can be with your sturdy feet,
how strong you are when you take your seat,
how kindness can alter the demands of time,
how many challenging mountains you will climb,
and how you carried on because you believed...
This is how impossibilities are achieved.
Hands, arms, ears, wings, minds, and eyes
need a heart full of hope in a world trying to cope."

The ant felt happy with this plan. She was delighted and elated; no longer felt defeated or ashamed of her existence. She knew that she mattered now, and her life suddenly felt completely brand new.

Vind

a mythical reality that is all mine

I am becoming one with the waters within me.

They tell me to remember to let go of the need for closure or I will get stuck waiting, wishing and hoping again in another cycle for answers that may not come because they feed on my spirit and bright hope.

They tell me to rise above their waves because it is okay to begin the dance of life again.

They tell me that in order to become more me I must embrace the qualities I noticed in others as part of me.

I suddenly understand the truth. I am what I see—the good, the shadows and the bad—the dragon, the mermaid, the unicorn, the dolphin, the phoenix, the swan, the owl, the eagle, the wolf, the rabbit, the panther, the lioness and the unknown are also a part of me.

I make the saddest stories come alive with magic.

What was given in the times I reached out and had to come back to myself holds a truth that is bigger than me. The Weaver allows such breaking to occur only when His plans are greater than what you face. This is why I keep walking.

The path I've chosen is not for the faint hearted and all that I am walking out of shouldn't stay with me any longer. They have become far too heavy to carry by myself. They long for their freedom and so I walk with them on their journey to release what was lost but found from the ink that will not stop its bleeding freely from my heart and into the world.

I am becoming one with the waters within me.

All I have in this moment is gratitude for what is left—my easy breathing, my ocean of love returning and my evolved gifts of light.

They are what I express to glorify my Father in Heaven who made me, who kept His word to hold me when it got dark and who helped me find the courage to lose everything of no value in order to face losing everything that would take me away from Him on this path.

I am a witness to the powerful way the Weaver uses the plans of others to gift you beauty that cannot be taken from you.

Most battles you'd find must be fought alone in order to be true to yourself, your dreams and who you want to be. By this I mean, you are not by yourself.

When anyone asks me why I am in love with Jesus, I tell them it is because He sees me in all my mess, shaping and becoming and loves me exactly where I am. He is and will always be my beloved Weaver. When I give Him everything that hurts, He teaches me how to create art with it—be it in storytelling, in poetry, in sketches or in creativity.

I used to keep the rawest parts of me a secret because I knew they were not ready for any of the hands I'd met so far.

There is only one and it will have to be the white stallion with wings of hope, faith and love called Vind.

He reminds me from time to time when I hesitate… He says, "Allow your ink the volume it needs to be heard in your space for it is the right time to be seen."

I am becoming one with the waters within me.

Home

I'll always find you

Fernweh is a word I associate with me; a wonderful, untranslatable German word that describes the feeling of homesickness for a faraway land or a place you have not visited. It's not the same meaning as wanderlust. It is a profound feeling, an unsatisfied urge to escape and discover new places tainted with a sort of sadness; like missing a place you've not experienced as opposed to lusting over it or desiring it like needing to wander. It is like seeking freedom and self-discovery without looking for security or a particular place. There are too many feelings wrapped up into this little word but to sum it all up, it always seems to say: Remember, the world is infinite but you can only have one home.

I am strong, tough, independent, strong-willed, bossy as the weather, and determined to be. I used to hold it together for many people but this was my lie because I was not strong at all but afraid, constantly pretending I was not.

I found trails less traveled and grabbed the hand of the Creator as tightly as I could, scared of slipping, yet always trying to be the pillar for everyone. I only ever fell apart when I stood beneath the silver stars in the night sky because then I knew I was not alone.

I am loved by people who are not always demonstrative. I feel sad when it feels like I am rejected. Sometimes, I don't mind because I know that I am loved and being strong suddenly doesn't seem too hard for me to be. But sometimes, I do mind.

If you are quiet, you might see me painting dreamily over my canvas or hear me singing a note or two. My eyes showcase things unspoken. I feel deep pain, hurt, and loneliness beneath the simple words of small talk.

My head tilts often to the side as I ponder mysteries that I have no clear answers to.

My ready laughter springs out of a mouth that often stays ribboned in silence as I observe the world about me.

I hear soft sighs and the gentle patter of the rain which lets me speak only in dreams to someone who I know will understand me.

You might think I live in a world of my own, but in reality, I frequently escape into the worlds of other people. I dance under moonlight when my spirit gets a bit loony.

I am passionate about humanity, the sand, waves, and about music that reveals the heart's desires.

I cherish deep memories that make me smile and cry secretly when no one watches me.

I yearn for the unknown to be revealed and wait impatiently for time to open its wrapped up treasures.

Inside, I bleed fountains of words and words and words. Drowning in these one day, I removed the lid. From the ashes on the ground, I found the wings of the phoenix and glided over the mountains, feeling the beat of the wind, the rhythm of my heart, and suddenly, all those words overflowed to meet the great oceans. Silent for so long, I found my moment to speak at last, to open a side rarely exposed to the world.

So if you notice me, the girl who seems aloof and reserved who smiles enigmatically, I hope you'll step a little closer, but be careful not to startle me for I might just decide to transform into a mermaid and disappear into the vast, stormy blue…

I am after all the Moon and water covers and protects me but no matter how lost you may be, I'll find you in the dark to sing songs of wild hope and light to your heart for you to see the path that leads straight back to where you belong.

Let Love In

knock, knock, knock

Let love pursue you.

Let love inspire you.

Let love pray for and with you.

Let love walk beside you.

Let love communicate from the past, the present, the future, the soul, the tongue, the heart, the spirit and body.

Let love learn who you are. Let love receive your heavy. Let love give to you. Let love accept you. Let love find you many times. Let love cook for you. Let love be flawed. Let love make mistakes. Let love be imperfect. Let love write poetry on your heart. Let love sing out of tune songs to you. Let love turn you into a muse. Let love be crazy about you. Let love study you. Let love create art that tells the world how much love loves. Let love invent languages. Let love fight with you. Let love be angry with you. Let love make up with you. Let love share what you can't carry. Let love be sad with you. Let love laugh with you. Let love touch you.

Let love hug you... extra, extra, extra long.

Let love kiss you... everywhere.

Let love be forgetful.

Let love show up for you when you need it.

Let love teach you vulnerability.

Let love make you grow wild in kindness, in bravery and faith.

Let love tend to your inner healing.

Let love bring out the child in you. Let love help you achieve your dreams.

Let love make traditions with you. Let love grow old with you.

Let love hope with you. Let love jump into your arms. Let love pick you up.

Let love make you smile. Let love worry about you. Let love be free.

Let love be selfless.

Let love flow.

Let love be. Anything. Everything.

Always, always, always, let love in because when you do,
you let Christ take the highest seat in the heart of all that you are.

Knock, knock, knock.

Let love in.

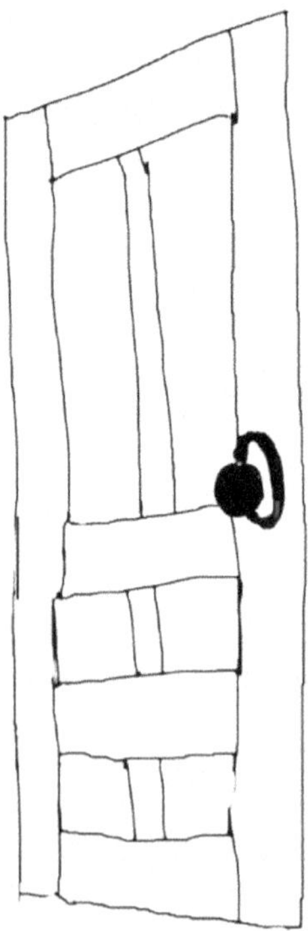

Lightning

your sparks enflame me

I know about drowning in limitless water
but what about drowning in fire?

What does a butterfly look like
when it gets hit by lightning?

Can it take this force of nature
and transform into a Phoenix?

Does it consume fire
or get consumed by it?

I didn't know
but I had to try.

Reena Doss

Farfalla

you have painted your wings

Spirende Farfalla, Emerging Butterfly,
spring awakens me…

I push the door to the new world open.

I let cramped wings stretch.

They have been growing,
learning how to dive
when the time comes to leave
the comfort of what I have known.

Gentle hands have helped me sew
what was lost and broken inside.

Dreams are awakening in the morning,
healing threads fasten themselves
into the emerald edges of my feet
and I am arriving home within.

Become

and may your light burn brighter

Stop overthinking,
Pearl in an oyster.

Travel wide and far,
Caterpillar of so many leaves.

Grow wild inside,
famished Chrysalis in your space.

Become you, dear Butterfly
with painted scars for wings.

Become you and soar into the sky.

Gather the stars and your silken dust.

Let the clouds uncover the Moon.

Much is waiting for you so just become…

Become

You.

Reena Doss

Derecho

you will reveal my grand love story

I am the butterfly in Monsoon,
unsheathing her wings,
realizing all that I am and all I can be.

I'm afraid but my desire to leave
my only known forever home
has become more stronger.

I love it with all my heart
but how odd to acknowledge
that I can no longer fit
within its once treasured walls.

I see the unicorn and dolphin
in chrysalises still.
I know one day they will become
butterflies with homes of their own;
but to let them discover
their freedom wings,
I cannot stay.

How hard it is to leave them…

I see the dragon and mermaid
gliding side by side…
Their faded wings have been stolen by time
yet how glad they should be
to see mine bloom

Knives press into my flesh unseen.
Am I wrong to leave them?

A voice I now recognize calls me;
I spread my wings, hesitating...

Reena Doss

Will they need me?
Perhaps.

Do they know how painful
this choice has been for me?
Perhaps not.

Will they miss me?
Yes, but only fleetingly.

The chrysalises will be too busy growing
and I will be happy witnessing their first flight,
just like others witness mine.

I am painfully aware that
this is not home right now
but a precious place
I can visit at any time.

As long as we all exist,
it is possible to glide into the past
and make new memories
but we cannot stay together
in stagnancy
or we will decay.

It is the way of nature.

Wings were not given to us
to stay on the ground.

This has always been my desire
when I was but a caterpillar
on an autumn leaf,
but now that the time has come....

Why does my heart break so loudly?

It tears the open sky and brings in the rain.

A storm has suddenly uprooted my safety
but a heart I recognized was found within.

It calls me now
and though a squall line of storms approach,
I must go to find its beat.

Butterflies avoid unclear weather
but my time of growth is now
and so I will fly
through this derecho thunderstorm
for love is an adventure
that begins with oneself.

I do not know if I will make it
but I will try,
even if my wings get torn.

Beauty is not all that I possess.
I am intensely brave,
I am immensely strong
I am resourceful enough
to find on my own
this heart that calls me
home.

Reena Doss

Wild Wolf

sing to the artic white moon

The art of my soul is a splash of colors
with hues and sighs, marigold emblems
of fire under the musical sky.

White Moon silhouette,
the wolf's pack protect my every move,
as I melt into the oceans of time
to discover the wonders beneath.

Mermaid butterfly,
sea urchin and space bird,
I am many parts uniting
as one voice inside me
and you know this
because you recognized me
before I did.

Reflections in a mirror,
we are the beginning and endless ache of us—
the healing and the unhealed, the shadows and the gray,
the death of the old and the transition into the new.
We are dancers in the dark, lovers of the heart,
musicians of the mind until we meet in the flesh
and unite with the light.

I am the wild
you never knew you wanted,
the wild you never believed existed
and the wild
you will never be able to explain.

You will not rest until I am
wrapped up in your forever arms.

Manifesto

to write, art and create

When I write poetry or prose, I escape into unfathomable worlds that exist between my pen and words while I lay back, enraptured by all that they reveal.

The seductive thrall I'm beholden to in the journey of these lines as they find each other like long lost friends, linking themselves into a permanent club hypnotizes and captures me within its moods of redemption and healing.

They shatter my beliefs constantly as they evoke a wild, almost instinctive knowledge in the mystical symbolism of God and His creation and I am left feeling overwhelmed by the magnitude of its nature, the way it slips and slides into every facet of my life.

I use the numbers—3, 7 and 13 frequently in all my written works to denote the Holy trinity, month, and day I was born with an odd mathematical compulsion to reinforce my existence and to map out the point I began this magnificent trail that has ignited my path constantly with lanterns of hope, faith, and love.

I enjoy the pace and rhythm of syllables, rhymes, and patterns because they allow the poet in me to release pent up emotions over everything and anything under the Sun and His celestial sky but most of all, I love not sticking to the norm by not following the conventions of prose and the forms of poetry or even the way I draw or sketch a piece of art.

To me, the skill of creating is like finding a part of your body you didn't know could function without your brain or heart or mind but is a semblance of unity when they produce together this magical ability that transforms what was once impossible into unimaginable possibilities.

I may stutter or cry as I jumble my words with speech but give me a pen and I'll show you how mountains will fly, how skies will walk, and how rainbows can shine forever in hearts that believe in its colors of humanity.

Wishes

that my inner child knew all along

I want to leave this world after doing something good.
Dance everywhere, wild, wild, wild flowers
I want friends to laugh at memories we've travelled in
Echo hope always, dear sunflowers
I want family to remember all I did to keep them safe
Black and white memories, sweet citric timeless weeds
I want my husband to rejoice knowing we lived well
There will only be you, my blue fire rose
I want my children to smile each time they think of me
Bring joy to the sad ones, my prancing dandelions
I want to exit this life with a legacy I am proud of
Fly into the horizons, bird of paradise
I want to meet my beloved Weaver with peace in my heart
Thank you for it all, especially, for the love I found in the unknown

I am a willow tree that loves her phases
a fallen birch yearning for the sun and moon to eclipse
twigs aching and drawn towards the deep

These are the seeds I planted deep in the pots
I kept upon the window sill of my inner home
I nurture them with faith, songs and kindness

Nobody knows how the flowers will grow
except the King of Kings,
Author and Master Commander
of space, time and distance.

Little Notes

Odds and ends are not random findings of matter,
they all have meaning and lead somewhere

The Pearl

1. Spiritual Perspective:

The creation of the Pearl is how God loves each of us—madly, deeply, and irrevocably. He gave this entire world to us, including His own son, so that we can have eternal life with Him. In God's eyes, we are loved individually as if each one of us were this amazing Pearl; no matter our history, our messes, and what causes us to suffer. Oysters know how to surrender their pain to the plan of God so they can transform into versions that are so beautiful, men dive into oceans searching for them. This becomes our true value when we see and acknowledge our worth in the price we were bought with—from the consequences of our own sins—the price being the most precious Pearl of all, Jesus Christ. (Reference - Matthew 13: 45-46 The Parable of the Pearl)

2. Scientific Perspective:

A Pearl is an immune response created by God to protect the oyster from external parasites who seek to injure it intentionally or unintentionally. The oyster's cells learn to quickly form a defensive sac around these painful occurrence/s. This sac then releases calcium carbonate and conchiolin protein which then builds up in layers to design an impermeable barrier which we consider a precious gem—the Pearl. But when this Pearl is discovered, it is the oyster whose shelf-life gets sacrificed. Though it is no longer needed, we cannot ignore it because its story of survival, grief, and loss gave birth to something extraordinary—the Pearl—that everyone notices immediately.

3. Mystical Perspective:

It is said that pearls are the oldest known gems in history. There is an intriguing legend that I like, regarding how a Pearl came into being—Whenever a single drop of rain falls from the Heavens, it becomes the heart of an oyster. The Pearl is symbolic to me because it resembles the Moon (whom I closely associate myself with). Additionally, the Moon can bring light to those in the dark (hence the black cover), but only through the Sun. It also has an affinity with water which can diversify its shape at any time.

As water (specifically, the ocean) is my favorite element (containing ether, air and fire), I often use its powerful terminology to express my thoughts, emotions, and feelings in my writing, creativity, and art. The knowledge that the Pearl is part of the ocean's self makes my joy in the mystery of unknown things more meaningful. Did you know that pearls are also known as teardrops of the Moon?

The Summer Leaf

I chose to paint a Leaf to represent my family because it has one of the most dynamic, obvious cycles of growth throughout all seasons. Each part of the Leaf I've drawn represents my family—my parents, my sisters, my brother in Heaven and I. I intentionally created a Maple Leaf because in Asia, it is an ancient symbol that represents the sweetness and wonder of love shared in daily life. To me, this is what it means to cherish family: I don't take family for granted because only we know the struggles, hardships, and sacrifices we've made on our own or together that have ultimately made us who we are, taught us how to love selflessly, and have kept us grounded. This is because we know that it is the Weaver who leads and holds us together in all things—great or small—as we continue to make a difference in each other's lives and in the lives of others. We are more than blood; different in shape, vision, and goals yet we are still each a part of the grand unravelling story of the Leaf.

The Color Green

During my life, I have aligned myself with different colors ranging from black, white, blue, red, purple, and now Green. Over the last three years as I began to settle into the woman I have fought to become, I discovered that I love Green the most. Green represents Hope, Restoration, and Eternal Life. For me, Hope leads to healing, joy, and possibilities, Restoration creates the ability to transition into new beginnings and the goal to attain Eternal Life for my soul (i.e., the ultimate victory over Death which is my driving motivation).

Autumn is my favorite season because it tells the story of growth, but it also holds that wonderful promise of Spring and Spring is fresh, beautiful, and Green. Green also symbolizes the breaking of chains and freedom from bondage.

The Archangel Raphael (meaning "It is God who heals" or "God heals" or "God has healed") whom I like for a number of reasons is associated with Green. His feast day was originally held on October 24th and is my father's birthday too.

This is why *Pearl On A Summer Leaf* was introduced last year in 2020 on this particular day at Ink Gladiators Press. *"The Lord is my Shepherd, I shall not want. He makes me lie down in green pastures…"* (Psalm 23) remains to this day my favorite psalm because I have witnessed my beloved Weaver Of The Celestial Sky fulfill this in my life over and over and over again until I fall to my knees, unable to handle the overwhelming outpouring of love that He showers over me freely as He handles my well-being so very carefully, firmly, and patiently.

Weather

Though July is the Summer month in the western world, it is also the Monsoon or rainy season in India. I have always thought it fascinating knowing that leaves are green in two different parts of the world—the ones that shine with the sun and the ones that glisten with the rain. I have always loved the rain. Why do I love it so much? Because I was born amidst a storm and the rain was the only thing that was left. From the time I came into this world, I have slept peacefully to the sound of falling rain. To me, it is the most lovely, calming, and comforting sound and you'd often find me near a window somewhere, writing or reading along with a steaming cup of coffee or tea. I don't remember a single birthday when the Weaver hasn't sent the rain for me. Even if He does not send it in the future, I know He'd remind me of it in some special way. These tiny details are a part of a love language shared only between Him and I and that make me realize how loved I am by the God of this Universe.

Numbers

Did you know that God added green to this beautiful world on the 3rd day according to the book of Genesis? **Pearl On A Summer Leaf**'s official publication date is the 13th of July 2021, though the Kindle got published two days earlier. This made the 11th of July 2021—the book's first journey into the world. Incidentally, I also turned 34 on the book's birthday which added up to 7. My friend, Shruti Sharma, also pointed out that this manuscript was first completed in 2018 which was 3 years after the first edition got published. And now, the expanded edition has been published 3 years later as you can see. I do love the numbers 3, 7, 8, 11 & 13 now and I feel so happy discovering how all this syncs up. God makes everything so perfect in ways I haven't expected. He is a jaw-dropping magician of the impossible, maker of all my wildest dreams and the greatest love of my life. He is a jaw-dropping magician of the impossible, maker of all my wildest dreams and the greatest love of my life.

Additional Jottings

1. *Essays:* Writing *Manifesto* was a direct response to a challenge conducted by my dear friend who is also a creative collaborator, poet and artist—Miriam Otto @miriamo77. I wrote *Home* in 2017. It would become a point of reference to me later on when I realized that I was a poet and had always been one. I just did not know at the time that my prose contained elements of poetic expression. I wrote *The Dragon, The Mermaid, The Pyramid, The Unicorn, The Dolphin, Three, Soul Footprints* and *Derecho* in late 2019 when I realized that I had to change my life's direction and discover the unknown path that had opened for me. I wrote *Your Purpose, Reign Fire, Vind, Lightning, Farfalla, Become, Wild Wolf* and *Wishes* after 2021 as I took more decisive steps towards my future.

2. *Metaphors:* I refer to God as the Weaver Of The Celestial Sky and use the metaphor of the Sun to represent Jesus Christ. I also play with the metaphor of the Weaver and the Sun when referencing the loml (love of my life) and nature with a very different significance (that's when I remove the capitals in the words) because no human being can be put on the same pedestal as God.

3. *Rainbows:* I love rainbows and the Pearl's layers are like tiny prisms that refract light so it appears as if the colors of the rainbow can be seen on the round surface of the Pearl.

4. *Anatomy:* The anatomy of the Summer Leaf symbolizes my family members. Each edge represents one of us. It also represents the month I was born. Its symbolism is closely interwoven with my faith, family, nature, and personal growth.

5. *Title:* The intro and end pieces under Birth, Sheltered & Cracked inspired the title—*Pearl On A Summer Leaf.* The original title was called *Egg On A Summer Leaf* until my uncle, Terence Rajah, who is an amazing editor, proofread a couple of my original poems in October 2018 and corrected my repetitive use of the phrase "pearl egg" to just "Pearl".

6. *Sign:* The gemstones closely associated with the sign of Cancer are the Pearl and Emerald.

7. *Nature:* Cancer is a water sign which is associated with the Moon. Based on the year I was born, the Rabbit is a fire sign which is also associated with the Moon. The oyster and crab have hard shells on the outside, but are soft on the inside just like a Turtle. The Moon is part of the night sky which is why I feel so deeply connected to the stars.

Acknowledgements

I am grateful for all of you

First and foremost, I want to thank my beloved Weaver for believing in my potential, teaching me professional level skills and preparing me for success. He is the God who truly makes the impossible possible. He did not once check my budget but measured my hard work and trust in Him. I am deeply humbled by His consistent faithfulness, unconditional love, and amazing grace that wraps around my entire being. This is why I dedicate every book of mine to Him first—**The Weaver Of The Celestial Sky.**

Next, I would like to thank my first family—**James, Preethi, David in Heaven, Michelle, Talitha**—because through my parents and sisters, I have extended family members (by blood, by marriage as well as those who consider us theirs) for gifting me with the circumstances to access, develop and use my first voices of writing, followed by art and creativity—that I now ride into with freedom. They were specifically chosen by the Weaver to be given to me for a reason, a season and a lifetime. The realms of adventures in various stages I've experienced while growing up with them has brought many of my stories to life in ways that I can now see as priceless.

I am so glad that I made you gather around on the **13th July 2021** (a minute before midnight on the 12th) to hit "publish" for the first edition, and of course, Papa hit the button before everyone could do it together but I am so glad that Shruti was there to witness and capture the memory. One day, I am certain you will appreciate that moment as timeless. I know I do.

Thank you to my Uncles—**Terence Rajah** for being one of the first people to read a few original pieces from this manuscript and for making great recommendations that helped me realize I needed to let my draft mature before thinking of publication and **Robin Doss**—for always gifting me with books to read during my growing years and for listening to me when I needed guidance on big decisions in my life.

Thank you to my (passed on) grandmothers—**Nana Agnes** and **Grandy Egypt** for inspiring me at different stages in my life.

Thank you to my godparents—**Margaretta Sarkar** and **Ashok Doss** who did your best to nurture my gifted voices by listening and staying curious whenever I talked to you about them.

So much gratitude to **Shruti Sharma** for volunteering to edit my first book in order to support my dream journey. She has been an amazing editor, whose eagle-eyed vision caught every mishap and whose professionalism kept my voice consistent throughout the book. As my best friend, she is already a treasure and I appreciate her for so many things, including encouraging me to post my work publicly on Instagram for the first time in 2018. Thank you for staying up with me, editing the first edition before it was released on the 11th of July 2021. I will not forget that for as long as I live.

Thank you also to my writer friend and colleague, dear **Magic Meghan Maggie Smith.** Thank you for making those few edit suggestions. I appreciate them very much.

Thank you to my friend, **Mrinalini Aryan,** who often stays quiet in the background but has been a good friend throughout the 30+ years that I've known her.

I want to acknowledge the support of **Miriam Otto** for collaborating with me on so many adventures these last 6+ years, for challenging me to write a manifesto (which I have included in the book) and for writing *Travellers for Life* with me. I even added a quote by Leon from that book. Thank you, dear **Miriam Otto @miriamo77** for being the first one to buy the kindle and paperback limited edition.

Also, grateful to **Jared Presser @forget_it42** who bought the hardcover to read it while on his vacation. Thank you, dear **Elle @5cand1e_lie5,** my friend from Instagram for buying the paperback. Also thank you to **Michelle Doss @mysticmichelle,** my sister for buying a couple of local copies to distribute to your friends.

Thank you to my sister, **Talitha Doss @colourmecrazy30** for taking pictures of the books I bought and posting on Instagram for me. A huge thank you to the five reviewers—**Shruti Sharma @shrutiscapes** and **Mrinalini Aryan @mrinalini8612,** thank you my dear friends for buying the paperback and sending me pictures of it. Thank you to my amazing friend and professional book reviewer—**Darya Silman** as well as **Geraldine Steele** and **Rupali Gore,** poetic colleagues I converse with from time to time but who kindly bought, read and left a review on Goodreads and Amazon for me.

I feel quite blessed to have a mountain range of love from friends who have been my inspiration, acted like family and who have personally influenced me at various stages in my life. They are: **Nutty Poopoo, Aunty Jo, Aunty Shobha, Marvin and Jennifer Molina, the Sharma family, Nikita Kapoor, Zulfiya Hamzaki, Yeshani Liyanage, Shruti Reddy, Grishma Gautam, Arundhati Deshpande, Medonguno, Nitisha Dias-Smith, Tanya Steele, Shalet Godwin, Sheena Menon, Virginia Victoria and Ritu Jose.** There are many others.

Some friends I have lost touch with because we chose different paths. Some I know I can talk to and with others, things reached an expiry date simply because we grew apart. Life does that to you and that's okay. I've learned to accept the lessons, hold on to memories and add new ones with the ones who don't make me feel like I have to stay guarded.

I am filled with lots of gratitude to the communities of Instagram, all of whom welcomed me with open arms and have encouraged my growth from poet to writer, artist, mental health advocate, co-author, collaborator, compiler, cover designer, publisher, book editor, epigrammatist, lyricist and now author (which was what I've wanted to be ever since I could write). This is why I wanted to celebrate my debut book—*Pearl On A Summer Leaf* with these phenomenal communities because they have embraced my true gifts and provided me with a platform to exist in my most authentic self. In all my adventures to reach this point, I have discovered the joy of mistakes. What appeared as out of place or like a puzzle of assorted pieces only grew infinitely more beautiful with each passing day as I took the detours to study each one a little more closely. Sometimes, just knowing what a wonderful circle of people the Weaver himself has sent, sends me into raptures of the sea of verse.

Tied with ribbons from the ocean and sent like the racing rivers, whispering trees and laidback mountains to find and let me know he is with me, **the love of my life** is a work of art, a pod of orcas navigating the wild and repeating words of love in ways that no one else could ever do except him. He is the key turning in the opening door of my heart because he has earned that right and has steadfastly accompanied me on the journey of bringing out my voices. Thank you for being the first to read the expanded edition, for recognizing and then, nurturing my voices. I know you don't like to be seen for the good things you do but in this case, I insist on giving you the credit for all the times you stood by me, for encouraging my dreams every day, for pouring fire into my hopes and for fighting my fears with me.

There is no one else that I can imagine being on this wonderful deep-rooted loving friendship filled with adventure than you. Thank you so much for all that you do to unwaveringly support me even though I can be a cactus with taking your help. I am so happy that you exist.

My heart overflows with so much hope, faith, and love in the possibilities of what is to come. Here's to being swept off my feet and into the mirrored heart of my future home one day!

Thank you, thank you, thank you!

Reena Doss

I'll find you in the dark because I'm the girl
who loves to stay lost amongst the midnight stars
caught up with moonbeams in a lantern,
trying to find my way back home.

-Runa Doss

Reena Doss

About the Author

Writing is Reena Doss' first voice of expression, followed closely by art and creativity. Through the encouraging platform provided by the Instagram community, she reclaimed her lost voices, evolved a few others and discovered new ones along the way. This has redeemed her trust that consistent Hope, Faith and Love in what is true ignites what is impossible to occur. Her adoration for her beloved Weaver, the Celestial Sky, Nature and her fellow Earthians has given her immeasurable courage to endure every season with a resilience born from battles overcome. Though she works at Ink Gladiators Press to primarily publish anthologies regarding important social concerns, world issues and mental health projects under the names—Our Earthians Community Group and Translations Of Hope, she also publishes her own books as well as helps self-publishers publish their manuscripts by using a few or all of her publishing skills (as needed).

Born in Calcutta with roots drawn from Chennai and Pondicherry, Reena Doss has lived most of her life in the south of India—Bangalore. Though she prefers traveling to far-off places inside her head, she sometimes ventures into the world that others call real.

You can try and catch her but it may not always be possible as she is generally off on adventures flying on phoenix wings, swimming into the deep with mermaids and chasing fiery dragons down for stories.

Please scan the following QR code to follow her on Instagram @reenadossauthor
www.reenadoss.com

Publications

throughout the years 2018-2024

Collaborations | Anthologies | Competitions | Events | Challenges | Interviews
Reviews | Cover Design | Interior Design | Editing | Formatting
Photoshop Artistic Elements | Compiling | Publishing | Poems | Essays
Prose | Epigrams | Lyrics | Photography | Digital Paintings

Note of Gratitude:

These publications wouldn't have existed without the wonderful people who have lifted me up in the currents of these years I spent walking on this dream path. It is exactly like following something you cannot see but know you would die if you chose any other. I am so deeply appreciative to all the people who have been a part of this journey over the last 6+ years. It's been exciting, with a lot of highs and a lot of lows. Thank you for walking with me and doing your best to be a part of all my adventures, despite being so busy in your own worlds. Thank you for standing by me through thick and thin. I am so grateful to my beloved Weaver, the loml, this wonderful community of creatives, especially my collaboration partners, authors, and strangers I have met, laughed and worked with. Thank you for believing in me.

2018

Birth Of A Poetess, Post from the first day of officially posting, Featured by A Voice From Far Away, Published on Instagram, September 13, 2018.

Twin Flames, the 6th piece in *Behind the Door,* an 8 Poet Blind Collaboration led and hosted by Abbey Forrest, Published on Instagram, October 20, 2018.

Ocean, the 7th piece in *The Explorer's Courtyard,* a 16 Poet Blind Collaboration led by Heather Millington and hosted by Abbey Forrest, Published on Instagram, November 1, 2018.

Crimson, the 4th piece in *Mind Monsters of Time,* a 14 Poet Blind Collaboration led by Heather Millington and hosted by Abbey Forrest, Published on Instagram, November 18, 2018.

Aliens, the 7th piece in *Invasion Invasion,* a 13 Poet Blind Collaboration led and hosted by Abbey Forrest, Published on Instagram, November 25, 2018.

Sober, A duo collaboration by Leon Jones and Reena Doss, Prompt by the Mingled Words Event with the community of Madpropslive, Hosted by Jared Presser and April Misschief, Published on Instagram, November 26, 2018.

The Elf & The Grinch: A Christmas Fable, A duo collaboration by Shruti Sharma and Reena Doss, Published on Instagram, December 26, 2018.

Mind Palace, the 6th piece in *Blind Soul Tendrils,* a 12 Poet Blind Collaboration led and hosted by Abbey Forrest, Published on Instagram, December 5, 2018.

Fans, the 9th piece in *The Heists Of Taco Tuesday,* a 12 Poet Blind Collaboration led and hosted by Abbey Forrest, Published on Instagram, December 11, 2018.

Mosquito Hunters, A duo collaboration by Shruti Sharma and Reena Doss, Published on Instagram, December 31, 2018.

2019

Grief, the 12th piece in *These Haunted Aspirations,* a 14 Poet Blind Collaboration led by Aamir and hosted by Abbey Forrest, Published on Instagram, January 19, 2019.

Cuckoo, the 6th piece in *Pieces To This Puzzle,* a 9 Poet Blind Collaboration led by Pooja Lahon and hosted by Abbey Forrest, Published on Instagram, January 29, 2019.

Nightmares, the 8th piece in *Insomnia,* a 10 Poet Blind Collaboration led and hosted by Abbey Forrest, Published on Instagram, February 11, 2019.

Hope, the 7th piece in *Flickered Visions,* a 9 Poet Blind Collaboration led and hosted by Abbey Forrest, Published on Instagram, February 19, 2019.

Time, the 10th piece in *The Coming Hour,* a 10 Poet Blind Collaboration led and hosted by Abbey Forrest, Published on Instagram, March 6, 2019.

Disasters, the 9th piece in *The Beginning,* a 12 Poet Blind Collaboration led by Linda Lokhee and hosted by Abbey Forrest, Published on Instagram, March 14, 2019.

Evolution, the 1st piece in *Hopeless Hope,* a 17 Poet Blind Collaboration led by Reena Doss and hosted by Abbey Forrest, Published on Instagram, March 30, 2019.

Elemental, A group collaboration by Lewis Feemster (Aether), Alex (Earth), Trey (Fire) and Reena Doss (Water), Published on Instagram, April 5, 2019.

Space, the 5th piece in *Final Frontier,* a 9 Poet Blind Collaboration led by Heather Millington and hosted by Abbey Forrest, Published on Instagram, April 18, 2019.

PenPals, the 8th piece in *Hand In Hand,* a 10 Poet Blind Collaboration led and hosted by Abbey Forrest, Published on Instagram, May 30, 2019.

New, the 6th piece in *Second Birth,* a 10 Poet Blind Collaboration led by Sunil Sathyendra and hosted by Abbey Forrest, Published on Instagram, June 3, 2019.

Completed 24 Poems at *The 2019 Poetry Marathon Challenge,* An international one day event, Hosted by Caitlin and Jacob Jans, Published live at The Poetry Marathon website, June 22 to June 23, 2019.

Timelines, the 12th piece in *For Love, We All Fight,* a 16 Poet Blind Collaboration led and hosted by Abbey Forrest, Published on Instagram, July 18, 2019.

Threads, the 8th piece in *The Possibilities,* a 8 Poet Blind Collaboration led by Timi Jolaoso and hosted by Abbey Forrest, Published on Instagram, July 20, 2019.

Dreams, the 3rd piece in *Somedays,* a 13 Poet Blind Collaboration led by Lainey and hosted by Abbey Forrest, Published on Instagram. It was also submitted to the anthology—Mind—to promote mental health awareness, July 23, 2019.

Pirate, the 20th piece in *A Parrot's Tale,* a 23 Poet Blind Collaboration led and hosted by Abbey Forrest, Published on Instagram, August 3, 2019.

Won a spoken word prize (*A Pack A Day* by Arthur J. Wilhelm) for *A Winter Romance Haibun* in *The Poetry Olympics Competition,* Judge was Janine @josameys.words, Hosted by Rani at Cement Covered Ink Quills (CCIQ), conducted by Poetry Olympics, Published on Instagram, August 18, 2019.

27 Forms at The Poetry Olympics Competition, Hosted by Rani at Cement Covered Ink Quills (CCIQ), conducted by Poetry Olympics, Published on Instagram, August to October 2019.

Starlight, A collum lune duet collaboration by Linda Lokhee and Reena Doss, Published on Instagram, September 13, 2019.

A Writer of the Heart (Poem)—*Ikigai: the reason for being,* Edited & Compiled by Janani V & Anupama CN, Published by Fanatixx, September 20, 2019.

Masqueraders, is the 3rd piece in *A Night of Decadance,* a 11 Poet Blind Collaboration led by Linda Lokhee and hosted by Abbey Forrest, Published on Instagram, September 27, 2019.

Awakening, the 1st piece in *Finding Gratitude,* a 10 Poet Blind Collaboration led by Reena Doss and hosted by Abbey Forrest, Published on Instagram, September 30, 2019.

Obstacles Unraveling (Poem)—*Misplaced Devotion: Works about Love,* Edited & Compiled by Jo Underwood, Published by Ambient Heights, October 31, 2019.

An Indian Sun Year (Poem) and *Sun Cycle Across Continents* (Contributor in Group Collaboration)—*Sun Cycle: Celebrating the World's Seasons*, Edited and Compiled by Sky Heywood and Poet Spotlight, Published by Teal Moon Publishing, November 2, 2019.

Christmas: The Greatest Gift Of All (Poem), *Easter: The Significance of The Cross* (Poem), *Pentecost: Anointing of the Holy Spirit* (Poem)—*The Diary of Festivities*, Edited & Compiled by Ishani Agarwal, Published by Notion Press, 6 November 2019.

The Elements and I (Poem)—*The 2019 Poetry Marathon Anthology*, Edited & Compiled by Jennifer Faylor, Published by The Poetry Marathon, November 15, 2019.

The Power and Responsibility of Words (Poem)—*Broken Hearts - Healing Words*, Edited & Compiled by A.B.Baird, Published by A.B.Baird Publishing, December 10, 2019.

Triangle, the 3rd piece in *Envy and Lovers*, a 10 Poet Blind Collaboration led by Timi Jolaoso and hosted by Abbey Forrest, Published on Instagram, December 19, 2019.

2020

Translations Of Hope (Poem)—*New Decade New Beginnings*, Edited & Compiled by Akshay Sonthalia, Published by Poets Choice, January 1, 2020.

Freedom In Hope's Wings (Poem) and *Somedays* (Contributor in Group Collaboration)—*Mind: A poetry anthology exploring mental health*, Edited & Compiled by Sky Heywood, Published by Poet Spotlight, March 15, 2020.

Cover (Digital Painting), Formatter, Book Designer, Narrative voice of Leon (Prose), Preface (Essay), 1 (Epigram), Leon and Miriam (Digital Painting)—*Travellers For Life: A duo poetic collaboration exploring the wonder of the unknown trail* by Miriam Otto and Reena Doss, Compiled by Reena Doss, Edited by Reena Doss, Miriam Otto and Preethi Doss, Published by Ink Gladiators Press®, May 11, 2020.

Cover (Digital Painting), Formatter, Book Designer, Narrative voice of Adela (Prose), Preface (Essay), *The Sun's Nature* (Poem) and Ike (Fan Art)—*A Forbidden Love: A duo poetic collaboration exploring the stigma of an office romance* by Linda Lokhee and Reena Doss, Compiled by Reena Doss, Edited by Shruti Sharma and Preethi Doss, Proofed by Reena Doss and Linda Lokhee, Published by Ink Gladiators Press®, May 13, 2020.

Cover (Digital Painting), Formatter, Book Designer, Narrative voice of Her (Prose), Preface (Essay), *Love* (Poem) 1 (Epigram) and Fire (Digital Painting)—*Love Is An Open Door: A duo poetic collaboration exploring the fundamental nature of true love* by Timi Jolaoso and Reena Doss, Compiled by Reena Doss, Edited by Preethi Doss and Reena Doss, Published by Ink Gladiators Press®, May 15, 2020.

Completed 24 Poems at *The 2020 Poetry Marathon Challenge,* An international one day event, Hosted by Caitlin and Jacob Jans, Published live at The Poetry Marathon website, June 27 to June 28, 2020.

Cover (Photoshop Manipulation), Formatter, Book Designer, 3 Featured Author Interviews, 8 Epigrams, The Weavers' Challenge and Introduction & Conclusion (Essays)—*Capsized: The Pandemic Lockdown,* Edited & Compiled by Our Earthians Community Group (Reena Doss), Introduction and Conclusion Proofed by Preethi Doss and Shruti Sharma, Published by Ink Gladiators Press®, September 13, 2020.

Editor, Formatter & Book Designer for *Viral Odes* by Sharron Green, Published by Ink Gladiators Press®, November 29, 2020.

Editor, Formatter, Cover Artist and Designer for *Godzillion Worlds* by Lorenza Palomino, Published by Ink Gladiators Press®, December 1, 2020.

The Pill Of Happiness (Poem)—*Poetry Pills: a prescription for goodness,* Edited & Compiled by Janani V & Anupama CN, Published by Paper Paints and Poetry, December 1, 2020.

Editor, Formatter & Book Designer for *Yellow Drops Of Stardust* by Miriam Otto, Published by Ink Gladiators Press®, December 6, 2020.

Editor, Formatter & Book Designer for *Monsoon Tales* by Shruti Sharma, Published by Ink Gladiators Press®, December 7, 2020.

Formatter, Book Designer, 2 Epigrams and a Letter—*Magical Jar: An artistic and poetic collaboration with seven friends* by Arun Chandra, Balaji V., Nishadi Thantrige, Miriam Otto, Ismet Diab, Shruti Jayakumar and Talitha Doss, Edited and Compiled by Reena Doss, Published by Ink Gladiators Press®, December 12, 2020.

2021

Cover (Photoshop Manipulation), Formatter, Book Designer, 7 book reviews, 41 Reviews of the authors' work, 12 interviews of Lockdown Perspectives, 7 Interviews of Hope Dealers from Translations Of Hope (TOH), The Stringing Words Challenge, Introduction and Conclusion (Essays), 13 Epigrams, 3 Featured Interviews of Authors and 43 Mini Q & As.—*The Fall And Rise Of Chimeras*, Edited & Compiled by Our Earthians Community Group (Reena Doss), Creativity Section Copyediting by Shruti Sharma, Introduction and Conclusion Proofed by Preethi Doss and Shruti Sharma, Published by Ink Gladiators Press®, January 7, 2021.

Editor, Formatter, Cover Artist and Designer for *Ink Quilled Thoughts* by Linda Lokhee, Published by Ink Gladiators Press®, January 21, 2021.

Editor, Formatter & Book Designer for *Scattered Syllables* by Linda Lokhee, Published by Ink Gladiators Press®, February 7, 2021.

Cover (Digital Painting), Formatter, Book Designer, 12 Epigrams, 72 Titles (Poem), *Tinman* (Photograph) *Gray Smoke* (Lyrics), *The Colors Seasons Wear* (Lyrics) and Introduction & Conclusion (Essays)—*Gray: We Hide Our Colors Within - Volume 1 (The Gray Volumes)*, Edited & Compiled by Our Earthians Community Group (Reena Doss), Introduction and Conclusion Proofed by Shruti Sharma, Published by Ink Gladiators Press®, February 23, 2021.

Editor, Formatter, Cover Artist and Designer for *Glistening Golden Circle* by Lorenza Palomino, Published by Ink Gladiators Press®, May 28, 2021.

Completed 24 Poems at *The 2020 Poetry Marathon Challenge*, An international one day event, Hosted by Caitlin and Jacob Jans, Published live at The Poetry Marathon website, June 26 to June 27, 2021.

Cover (Photoshop Manipulation), Formatter, Book Designer, *Come Find Me* (Poem), *A Bizzare Limerick* (Poem), *Sevenling Horror* (Poem), *A Shakespearean Sonnet Of Farewell* (Poem), 2 Epigrams and Introduction & Conclusion (Essays)—*The 2021 Form Runners & Inventors Collection*, Edited & Compiled by Our Earthians Community Group (Reena Doss), Published by Ink Gladiators Press®, September 13, 2021.

Editor, Formatter & Book Designer for *The Essence Of Chaos* by Timi Jolaoso, Published by Ink Gladiators Press®, October 17, 2021.

Editor, Formatter & Book Designer for *Dormiveglia* by Emma Major, Published by Ink Gladiators Press®, December 7, 2021.

2022

Editor, Formatter & Book Designer for *Poetscapes* by Shruti Sharma, Published by Ink Gladiators Press®, January 13, 2022.

Editor, Formatter & Book Designer for *Lights Stuck On Red* by Emma Major, Published by Ink Gladiators Press®, January 18, 2022.

Cover (Digital Painting), Formatter, Book Designer, *Ripped Wings* (Prose) and Introduction & Conclusion (Essays)—*Name Your Demons: Meeting Your Bleeding Wounds (Unchaining Freedom Trilogy Book 1),* Edited & Compiled by Our Earthians Community Group (Reena Doss), Introduction and Conclusion Proofed by Preethi Doss, Published by Ink Gladiators Press®, May 14, 2022.

Cover (Digital Painting), Formatter, Book Designer, Stagnant Critic (Prose) and Introduction & Conclusion (Essays)—*Fight Your Demons: Procrastinating Your Inner Healing (Unchaining Freedom Trilogy Book 2),* Edited & Compiled by Our Earthians Community Group (Reena Doss), Introduction and Conclusion Proofed by Preethi Doss, Published by Ink Gladiators Press®, May 14, 2022.

Cover (Digital Painting), Formatter, Book Designer, *Love Of My Life* (Prose) and Introduction & Conclusion (Essays)—*Conquer Your Demons: Embracing Your Victorious Scars (Unchaining Freedom Trilogy Book 3),* Edited & Compiled by Our Earthians Community Group (Reena Doss), Introduction and Conclusion Proofed by Preethi Doss, Published by Ink Gladiators Press®, May 14, 2022.

Editor, Kindle Formatter & Book Designer for *Wildfire & Magic* by Miriam Otto, Published by Ink Gladiators Press®, July 20, 2022.

2023

Cover (Photoshop Manipulation), Formatter, Book Designer, 12 Epigrams, 72 Titles (Poem), *Tinman* (Photograph) *Gray Smoke* (Lyrics), *The Colors Seasons Wear* (Lyrics) and Introduction & Conclusion (Essays)—*We Hide Our Colors Within: Uncaging The Phoenix*, Edited & Compiled by Our Earthians Community Group (Reena Doss), Introduction and Conclusion Proofed by Shruti Sharma, Published by Ink Gladiators Press®, May 31, 2023.

Co-Editor for *The Briny Sea Of Poetry* by Brandy Lane, Published by Where Beautiful Inks LLC July 25, 2023.

Editor for *Talking To The Moon* by Brandy Lane, Published by Where Beautiful Inks LLC, July 31, 2023.

Editor for *Who Casts A Spell On Us* by Miriam Otto, Independently Published, September 6, 2023.

Editor, Formatter, Cover Artist & Book Designer for *Oceans 7* by Ismet Diab, Independently Published, September 18, 2023.

2024

Cover (Digital Painting), Formatter, Book Designer, 8 Epigrams, The Challenge Collection and Introduction & Conclusion (Essays)—*The Weavers' Challenge - Book 1: Capsized: The Pandemic Lockdown (The Challenge Collection)*, Edited & Compiled by Our Earthians Community Group (Reena Doss), Introduction and Conclusion Proofed by Preethi Doss and Shruti Sharma, Published by Ink Gladiators Press®, January 23, 2024.

Editor for *Where Beautiful Loves II by* Brandy Lane, Published by Where Beautiful Inks LLC, January 28, 2024.

Editor, Formatter & Book Designer for *Willing Words* by Sharron Green, Independently Published, February 1, 2024.

Cover (Digital Painting), Formatter, Book Designer, The Challenge Collection, Introduction and Conclusion (Essays), 9 Epigrams and 41 Reviews of the Authors' work—*The Stringing Words Challenge - Book 2: The Fall And Rise Of Chimeras (The Challenge Collection)*, Edited & Compiled by Our Earthians Community Group (Reena Doss), Proofed by Shruti Sharma, Published by Ink Gladiators Press®, March 4, 2024.

Ink Gladiators Press®

Publishing and promoting warriors on life's battlefield

We serve the community of creatives as a whole. We love to publish, promote and preserve the voices of authors, writers, artists, poets, lyricists, photographers, philosophers, editors, designers, storytellers, mental health advocates, communities and creators.

Our aim is focused on a vision where authors, professionals and creatives can grow together by contributing their heart songs to humanity as gifts of inspiration where reality can be built through the art of dream-making. We look forward to welcoming your voices, their expressions and inviting them to make a home with our Ink Gladiator family through our anthologies, workshops and other supportive avenues. Not only do we offer A Hand To Hold Publishing where we recommend professional freelancers to help you on your publishing path, we also review and recommend publications that we enjoy reading so feel free to email us about your books before sending them to us in the format you are most comfortable with.

When we work together with faith, hope and love, everything is possible. We appreciate your love for reading and for being a part of our journey! Thank you for being here.

For any inquiries, please email us at contact@inkgladiatorspress.com.

We remain at your service,
Ink Gladiators Press® Team
www.inkgladiatorspress.com

Please scan the QR Code
to follow us on Instagram @inkgladiatorspress

To those who remain true to themselves,

to those who create magic wherever they go

and for those who sit beside the hurt when everyone else leaves,

Art will always immortalize you.

www.ingramcontent.com/pod-product-compliance
Lightning Source LLC
LaVergne TN
LVHW052206200726
843508LV00015B/1582